Jarawa
The Struggle Continues...

JARAWA

The Struggle Continues...

Dr. Pronob Kumar Sircar

AKANSHA PUBLISHING HOUSE
NEW DELHI • GUWAHATI • VISAKHAPATNAM

AKANSHA PUBLISHING HOUSE
4649-B/21, Ansari Road
Darya Ganj, New Delhi - 110 002
Ph.: 23263193 / 9811582579 / 09435116718
Fax: 011-23263193
Email: ektabooks@yahoo.com
www.akanshapublishinghouse.com

Jarawa: The Struggle Continues...

First Published 2011
ISBN 978-81-8370-261-4

[The responsibility for the facts stated, conclusions reached etc., is entirely that of the author. The publisher is not responsible for them, whatsoever.]

PRINTED IN INDIA

Published by Akansha Publishing House, New Delhi and Printed at Harmain Offset Press, Delhi.

To

My Grand Father

Rajani Ranjan Sircar

(1909-1979)

Contents

Preface

During the infancy stage of my research and study of the island tribes it was beyond my imagination about coming out of the Jarawas from their mainstream. That time (1994) no one had any idea of the possibility of their coming out and assimilation with the outsiders in villages and on road in broad daylight. After few years, I obtained the degree of Doctor of Philosophy and returned to my home island and to my surprise found that the Jarawas had come out of their abode forests and the things had shockingly been changed. After a long shoe rubbed efforts I got the swinging opportunity to join the Andaman Adim Janjati Vikas Samiti, Port Blair and to work among the little contacted Jarawas. Since then I never looked back and had a long stint amidst the Jarawa. The AAJVS established in March 1976 is the only authorized body under the aegis of the Andaman and Nicobar Administration to implement all the welfare schemes for the primitive tribes of the islands. As an employee of the AAJVS the extremely interesting period I spent with these ancient, rare and unique tribes has become the most memorable part of my life.

As an islander I personally realized very closely that the villagers living around the Jarawa Reserve in general are acrimonious, critical, and exasperated about the Jarawas. They know very little about the Jarawas' glorious history of struggle to save their motherland. I feel from core of my heart very sad when a villager speaks bitterly on the Jarawas for their killing of outsider or entry into a village. The evidential fact is that the poachers constantly compelled them to continue their trend of killing and attacks as revenge or self-defense. Now the Jarawas are voluntarily coming to contact the people as result of their mainstream friendship with the outside world further leading to their behavioural and material changes. This has further opened all the doors and windows for the fear-free poachers. Now a much reversed scenario has been emerged. Now the Jarawas are on road and village points while the poachers are freely doing their business in their reserve. The closure of Andaman Trunk Road of the reserve portion shall undoubtedly promote the growth of and protect the Jarawas, the virgin forest, the rich and near threatened flora and fauna, other terrestrial resources and the natural eco-systems of the islands. We, the so called civilized people have a genuine responsibility to save our threatened surrounding world.

Now, the Jarawas are under arguable transformation. They are passing through the most uncertain period in their history of thousands of year. The poaching has been one of the greatest threats to their survival. The poachers, tour operators, boatmen, fishermen and many others are in commercial rush to spice the JARAWA TOURISM and earn profits. Both the Andaman Trunk Road and the west coast have become the ground for such ventures. These have uprooted the fact that the initial result of the 'Outside Contact' has been geared up and multiplied leading to a complex situation which demands that we from time to time should closely observe and check the movement and activities of the tour operators and their vehicles, local boatmen, fishermen and villagers. The lodges, hotels, resorts and villages may be the ground for such observations. We cannot avoid the concrete fact that with the tide of times a strong network and mechanisms have been built around by offenders to promote the Jarawa Tourism and other acts of poaching. The burning issues pertaining to the population growth and village expansions are also standing on the line of subject. Thus the pressure on the Jarawa from all corners is on rapid increase. On the other end it is appalling that even after more than a decade of their mass contact with us we are still undecided exactly what to do with them. Some people say – push them to forest and some admit – No ! Bring them to mainstream. Through this book I am not trying to give final answers. I am just opening some doors for a deeper insight.

The present situation demands that before we spend time in search of Original Jarawa and their history, we realizing pulse of the situation should analytically review the present Jarawa problems to find an undisputable solution. The study of race and racism and anthropological study as preferably practiced few decades ago the human measurement from weight, height, proportion of limbs, noses, skulls, ears, breasts, buttocks (styteopygia), and other parts of the body to earwax, body smells, and nasal mucus have no meaning for the present Jarawas if we do not understand their basic need of now and do not protect their resources at the ground level. The researchers should locate themselves at a point between the Jarawas and the non-Jarawa settlers to construct a workable mechanism which may help the authority (Andaman and Nicobar Administration) to deal with one of the most focused present problems i.e. increasing contact between the Jarawas and non-Jarawas and exploitation of their (Jarawa) resources. I am sad enough that to a large number of local people the Jarawa means 'Problem'. Many people stepped further and advocated for bringing them into school and resettle them on a separate island. Their unfair ideas vary from one to another. The Jarawas are not the stray cows to push them back or not dogs to kick them out and not the TARZEN men to bring them into a HUMAN ZOO. To such people the simple and domestic question should be asked- whose land is this? And this is their big and open heart that these innocent people don't have the concept "this is yours and this is mine".

Apart from giving the essential references majorly historical, systematically compiled taking a long time, this book is an attempt to narrate my own experiences as an AAJVS worker with the amiable Jarawas, perhaps for the first time by a field worker of the AAJVS. The views and opinions placed in this book are not official but purely of myself and I take the utmost responsibility of anything emerged out of the materials published in this book. The book mirrors the crux of the present situation concerning the Jarawas unfolding the insidious and mysterious parts of the Jarawa Life. Above any noticed mistake, this work may be helpful to construct a platform for a fair understanding about the Jarawa aspects and to provide a workable ground for the others. I have written this book for both the ordinary and the thinking person. And, every ordinary man is a thinker. Significantly I find this book an incomplete one which awaits with patience the valuable suggestions/comments of the readers.

It is not so hard to believe that they are unique and purely innocent human beings who want to live on their own. We should love their world with all its imperfections and good aspects. If we go for even a pin work in the name of their welfare or development without having their consent ignoring their untold ultimate human appeal that would certainly be a grave mistake.

— Dr. Pronob Kumar Sircar

Acknowledgements

At the outset I sincerely thank to some officers of the Andaman and Nicobar Administration, staffs of the AAJVS and Directorate of Tribal Welfare for their co-operation in my work. I am also indebted to Shri Som Naidu, Former Executive Secretary of AAJVS, for his inspiration and cooperation to me during my work among the Jarawas. I am also thankful to some senior activists Shri Pankaj Sekhsaria, Prof. Vishvajit Pandya, Shri Samir Acharya, Late Govind Raju, Shri S A Awaradi, Shri Manish Chandi, Stephen Corry, Shri K.B.Saxena, Prof. R.K. Bhattacharya, and many others for their previous works on the Jarawas which further inspired and helped me accelerate this journey. Few members of them do not know me but I know them through their remarkable pieces of work.

This work is done for them and through them. I personally pay my salutary respect to the Jarawa members for their love, care and cooperation.

I am highly indebted to Akansha Publishing House, New Delhi who took very special care and interest in publishing this book at time.

At this juncture, I remember my maternal uncles Late Nirmal Chandra Bose, Shri Anil Kumar Bose, Shri Sunil Chandra Bose, my elder brothers Shri Ashis Sarkar, Shri Pradeep Sarkar, my sister Rekha Bhattacharya, my wife

Parameet Sircar and my friends for their constant encouragements and extending all supports to me.

The father and the mother are authors of one's being; and there is no one that deserves such reverence as the mother. On this auspicious occasion, I remember my mother Joythsna Sarkar and my father Shri Swadesh Bandhu Sarkar for their....I have no words...And I know if, I please them, gratify the earth herself.

Dr. Pronob Kumar Sircar

1

The Introduction and History

Blessed with beauty and exciting history the Andaman and Nicobar Islands in two separate groups of islands viz. Andamans and Nicobars are populated by different ethnic groups including some rare human races of the world living under very dissimilar conditions, each with its own problems and prospects. The nation's great freedom fighter Netaji Subhas Chandra Bose named these two groups of islands as 'Shaheed Dweep' and 'Swaraj Dweep' for their glorious history of the freedom struggle and sacrifices of the martyres. On a globe looking like tiny specks in an arc in the water of Bay of Bengal the Andaman and Nicobar groups comprising of islands, islets and rocks are located at a distance of more than 1000 kilometers from the Indian mainland. These islands have now tremendous scope for development of international tourism and fisheries. The Andaman and Nicobar archipelago is situated in the Bay of Bengal between 6 degree and 14 degree North latitudes and 92 degree and 94 degree East longitudes. The five major islands with other tiny islands are separated by narrow straits and creeks forming 'the Great Andaman' consist of a mass of hills enclosing very narrow valleys, the whole covered by dense tropical forests.The hills rise, to a considerable elevation: the chief heights being of

Saddle Peak in the North Andaman, Mt. Diavolo behind Cuthbert Bay in Middle Andaman, Mt. Koiob, Mt. Harriet and Cholunga range in south Andaman and Ford's Peak in Rutland Island. Despite their coral reefs, most Andaman islands themselves are not of coral origin. Instead they are the peaks of a drowned mountain range running from Cape Negrais in the Arakan Yoma Range of Myanmar to Achin Head in Sumatra. The older rocks are early Tertiary or late Cretaceous. The newer rocks are in Ritchi's Archipelago chiefly, and contain fossils of radiolarians and foraminifera. The coasts of the Andamans are deeply indented being surrounded by mangrove swamps. The chief harbours are Port Blair, Port Meadows, Colebrooke Passage, Elphinstone Harbour (Homfray's Strait), Stewart Sound, Port Cornwallis, Temple Sound, Interview passage, Port Anson or Kwangtung Harbour, Port Campbell, Port Mouat and Macpherson Strait, etc. The islands with tropical hot and humid climate with abundant rains are bestowed with luxuriant flora and fauna. The islands are sheltered by the 60 million year old Indo-Malayan tropical rain forests, a single hectare of which shadows thousands of species of plants and animals. The huge trees with umbrella leaves are so densely grown together that hardly any ray of sun drops on the ground. But I should not say that the forest in these islands are now 100% sacrosanct. The forests in Andamans are undoubtedly facing a major threat from the poachers engaged in logging operations. In a report to the Department of Environment in 1983, consultants Dr. S.C. Nair and Dr. S. Santhi have revealed that forest cover in north Andaman has declined from 96% to 21%. Now one can guess how much worst the present situation is. The faunal elements of these islands bear with both Indo-Malayan and Indo-Chinese affinities due to the geographic proximity of those landmasses. The animal life is generally deficient throughout the Andamans. The absence of large mammals and presence of endemic fauna and flora is an interesting aspect of their composition. This paucity of animal life seems inconsistent with the theory that the islands were once connected with the mainland. There are 284 species of birds found in the islands. Few of them are threatened to the world while many of the birds are endemic to these islands. Out of 1340 species of birds recorded from Indian subcontinent, 21 % are found in these islands. The Andaman and Nicobar Islands are said to be located on a tectonic plate and is referred to as Andaman Plate by Dasgupta (1993) and Burma Plate by Currey et al. (1982). This tectonic plate which forms the ridges of the islands is sandwiched between the Indo-Australian Plate on the western side and the Eurasian Plate in the north and the east. The Indian lithosphere on the western side subducts below the Andaman (Sunda) Plate (Fitch 1970, Dasgupta and Mukhopadhyay 1993, Rajendran and Gupta 1989).

The tribal population of the Andaman and Nicobar Islands as per 2001 census is 29469, which is 8.27% of the total population. In addition to the mongoloid tribes viz. Nicobarese and Shompen, the Andaman and Nicobar Islands are the homes of some ancient, rare and unique Negrito tribal groups viz. the Great Andamanese, the Onge, the Sentinelese and the Jarawa.

They call themselves 'ANG' but the world knows them as 'JARAWA' called by their neighbouring Aka-bea group of the Great Andamanese tribe means 'Stranger'. The Jeru band of the Great Andamanese calls them as 'Kontoka' means 'the man who shoots arrow'. One of the most ancient people of the present world 'the Jarawa' live in the world famous rain forests in limited parts of the Andaman Islands.

The recently contacted rare tribes live in the forest of the Andaman Islands have been considered as living human heritage of the entire world. They have always been a subject of mystery and curiosity for the outside people. Though many explorative and research works have been conducted on them which are of course workable, for the readers this is my one simple effort to highlight some sensitive aspects of the Jarawas on basis of my own field experiences that are essential in understanding deeply what they need, what they say, what can we do for them, and the crux of the present situation. They are now around 362. The Jarawa Reserve after inclusion of the medical wards has been increased from 847 to 1028 sq. kms. The exclusive marine resource base has also been increased by declaring coastal water upto 5 km from High Tide Line as Tribal Reserve. An administrative policy has also been finalized in 2004. Apart from the constitutional safeguards, these are one of the few steps underlined for the Jarawas. But the ground realities reveal that we need more constructive works to do reducing a long talk on them.

At the very outset I recollect those childhood days when we children at Port Blair used to run after two types of people in curiosity. One is Europeans for their physical features differ from us Asians and the second is native black people called 'junglee' in local parlance. I do not know exactly when I started growing with anxiety towards the native people of the Andaman islands. Was that the time when I was eleven and heard about a Jarawa attack on few fishermen ? or when I saw a disfigured dead body of a man in Jarawa attack at Tirur at the age of thirteen or fourteen? or when I saw Ramu for the first time? Ramu, an Onge man was employee in the Directorate of Shipping Services who used to be quite usually seen near the Marine Gate at Port Blair just at one km distance from my house situated at Anarkali village. He was always seen quite different from the other people for his ill fitted clothes, the jet black skin but attractive, the small curled woolly hair, and his big and attractive eye balls. Whenever I saw him my growing mind asked me several questions in curiosity. But there was nobody to answer my mute questions. Sometimes I saw the people teasing him and throwing 'chewing gum' on his curly hair without minding the sentiments of the tribal member. Nobody came forward in compassion towards the innocent native. These pictures painted in my child brain further really worked. After a long passage of time, I recollected the Ramu episodes during my research in 1994 for M.Phil. degree from Dr. Babsaheb Ambedkar National Institute of Social Sciences, Mhow (Indore). I without a hitch selected the vulnerable Onge tribes to work on their subsistence economy and finally I obtained the degree of Master of Philosophy. This further led me to complete my Ph.D. on "Impact of the Development Programmes on the Primitve Tribes of Andaman and Nicobar Islands". During this period of study and research my knowledge and understanding abut the island tribes began growing greedily. Meanwhile under a project from Ministry of Home Affairs, Govt. of India I had to conduct ethnographic study on the Baiga tribes of Mandla, Shehdole, Balaghat, Sidhi and Jabalpur in Madhya Pradesh. The Baiga tribes are also a neglected people in their own villages. Their cultural entity is under a great threat. Inspite of the fact that their conditions are different from the Andaman tribes, all the tribes of this nation commonly stand with a single voice for want of the justice and additional care.

After completion of my study I returned back to my home land (Port Blair) with the great enthusiasm to work on the tribal people on whom I did my doctoral thesis work. As it was my first and last choice I joined the Andaman Adim Janjati Vikas Samiti, Port Blair which is the only organization purely undertaken by the Andaman and Nicobar Administration to look after the primitive tribal communities of the islands. Thanks to Shri Somnaidu, the then Executive Secretary, AAJVS (now one of the experts concerning the Jarawas), who deputed me frequently on patrolling duty in the Jarawa areas at the initial stage to help me to understand about the Jarawa situation and the changing trend of the Jarawas. Gradually my curiosity greedily increased towards the little known Jarawa tribes who just started to come out to contact the outside people voluntarily. For the time being my ambition to work on the Onges slightly drifted towards THE JARAWA for their creating one of the most challenging social situation in their history of contact with the outsiders.

The origin of the tribes remains shrouded in mystery today despite countless attempts made by ancient travelers, historians, anthropologists and government officials to unveil their roots. Who were the first people to set foot on these islands? Where did they come from? Did they all arrive in one go or in succeeding migratory waves of small groups? How are the tribes here related to population groups elsewhere in the world? Researchers are in continuous attempt to reach answers. The current consensus is that modern human originated in Africa and spread to other countries sometime between 50,000 and 1,50,000 years ago. Some experts have adopted OUT OF AFRICA theory suggesting that the Negrito tribes on the Andaman and Nicobar Archipelago may be the direct descendants of the first of modern humans who migrated out of Africa. The Africa was indeed the original homeland of our species is suggested not only by an independent molecular study by Luingi Luca Cavalli-Sforza at Standford University but also by the archaeological record in the form of bones and stone implement. No one has been able to answer the question with any degree of accuracy, as to how and when the Jarawa came to the Andamans. The archaeological study of kitchen-middens of Andamanese revealed that the Negritos were present atleast 2000 years ago in the Great Andamans. It is believed that the Jarawas had arrived after the Great Andamanese in these Islands on basis of the fact that the word "Jarawa" derived from the Great Andamanese Aka-bea language means 'Stranger' means those who came later. Gradually in course of the explorative oservations and findings more than ten to twelve groups territorially separated from each other were identified and grouped in one 'the Andamanese' later joined by Jarawa and/or Jungil(tribes of Rutland Island). In spite of some important scientific findings, the knowledge about the origin and migration of the primitive tribes is still dissatisfying. Now the mysterious Jarawas are about to undergo genetic scrutiny. From the studies on their genes, scientists hope to find all the desired answers about their origin, migration and genetic distribution and of many other unsolved questions. The genomic research, they believe will also help the tribes themselves for their protection and growth through the new versions of science.

The oldest but an obscure description about the islands' existence in the Bay of Bengal is available in the Ptolemy's Agathon daimonos Nesos of second century AD followed by available notes and travelogues of old travelers and explorers continuous from the seventh century A.D.; and the islands regularly appear in some shape or other on maps of these regions from the middle ages onwards. It is still not clear whether any of the names of the islands given by Ptolemy ought to be attached to the Andamans. The islands first appear distinctly in the Arab notices of the 9th century and later mentioned by Nicolo Conti (1440), Cesare Federici (1569) and Captain A. Hamilton (1727). The works and descriptions of many persons particularly J. Ritchie, Archibald Blair, Frederick J. Mouat, R.H.Colebrook, J.H.Helfer, Oscar Malitte, E.H. Man, H.F.Corbyn, B.Ford, J.N.Homfray, G.E. Dobson, Maurice Vidal Portman(1861-1935), H.S.Man, J.P.Walker, J.C.Haughton, R.C.Tytler, T.Cadell, R.C.Temple, A.R. Radcliffe Brown, and Von Elickstedt etc. helped us to know a handful history of the Andaman islanders. In 1788 the East India Company commissioned the Great Surveyor, Archibald Blair to start a settlement on the ordinary lines, to which convicts were afterwards sent as labourers. He was an employee of the Bombay Marine. He worked in Calcutta (now Kolkata) before he was sent to the Andamans. In 1789 a meeting of the British Governor-General in Council took place in Calcutta and as decided in the meeting he was sent to colonize the islands to get a safe harbour from where they can check the movement of Malayan Pirates and to help shipwrecked people and to build a base for emergency situation. He left Calcutta with two ships viz. Elizabeth and Viper. After completion of his survey from Andamans to remote volcanic island called Barren Island he returned back to Calcutta on 22-04-1789 to submit his report to the authority. The Commander, Army Captain Alexander Kyd appointed his lieutenants to conduct further surveys in the islands. He returned on 28-09-1789 in the island and then first penal settlement was established in the island. The spot he selected for his residence was 'Mark Island' which is now called 'Chatham Island'.

Initially there was no plan to establish a penal colony. Some convicts were taken as unpaid labourers. That time the present Port Blair was named as 'Port Cornwallis'. On 16-10-1792 the final order was given for shifting of the settlement from Port Blair to Port Cornwallis, North-East Harbour which is now called the Diglipur. Later on 05-11-1792 Chatham settlement was shifted to the North-East harbour. In March 1793 the local command was handed over to Captain Kyd. Several skirmishes and encounters took place between the island aborigines and the British. The island witnessed from time to time the great valour and gallantry shown by the native belligerents (Andamanese Negrito) to drive out the invaders. The first penal settlement was abandoned in May 1796 because of its malarious environment and other hampering circumstances on the lives of settlers and for East India Company it was very expensive to manage the things and maintain the colony under the contemporary circumstances. The convicts were transferred to Penang and the settlers returned to Bengal.

The first recorded Jarawa reference was made in 1790. Lieutenant Robert Hyde Colebrook made a survey around the Andamans in 1789-90 under Captain Kyd. During that period and after that for a long time the world knew only about one tribe the Great Andamanese. Colebrook himself had no idea about the existence of another tribe the Jarawa. But Colebrook as he was very much interested to work in the field of linguistics, kept continued the collection of tribal words whenever got opportunity. One day Colebrook found few tribes with canoes near the present Dundas Point. Some words collected by him were later found to be of Jarawa language. This leads the fact that the Jarawa had canoes about 200 years ago but during the second penal settlement there were only Great Andamanese near the harbour area but no Jarawa surprisingly. The entire area around the harbour including the North Bay was occupied by the Great Andamanese tribes.

There are more evidences which advocate the fact that the Jarawas had canoes:

" On 16th November 1884 Portman's expedition anchored near the Cinque Island when they saw some smoke coming out of the jungle. Three canoes of the Jarawas found there, were kept on board. Oldham the in-charge of operation captured and brought nine of them to Port Blair and after a long stay they were taken back and made free"(Pronob Kr. Sircar: 2004) .

Those who do not know exactly the history of Jarawa or do not understand the tribal way of defence generally called the Jarawa 'unfriendly people'. The history tells that before they came unfriendly towards the outsiders they came in contact of the outsiders with friendly gesture on several-recorded occasions. Colebrook in the said contact was able to collect some Jarawa words with no skirmish. Portman also tested the words collected by Colebrook to be of the Jarawa language. It is evident that the aborigines with whom

Colebrook and Lieutenant Blair and others were on friendly terms included the Jarawas of the South Andamans. Further more, in all probabilities, those taken to Calcutta in 1790 too were the friendly Jarawas.

It is very remarkable that the penal settlements established in the Andamans two times in 1789 and in 1858. But it doesnt mean that the islands were left alone in between the two settlement periods. The islands were frequently visited for variuos purposes. Many of the visitors had been murdered. One of them Dr. Helfer, a Russian Geologist who was killed at Port Cornwallis in 1839. The natives of Nicobars were also continuing their attacks on the invaders. In 1839 a pilot of a vessel and his crews were attacked. In 1844 Capt. Caw was killed at Camorta. Such attacks were continued even in 1866, when Brig Fateh Islam and about 21 crews were murdered by the Nicobarese. In 1849 two ships 'Emily' and 'Flying Fish' were wrecked off the west coast of the Andaman islands.The aborigines had killed the Second Officer of the 'Emily'. In 1855 three sailors of the ship 'Fyze Baksh' of Moulmein were murdered and four others were wounded by the Andamanese. On failing of the first penal settlement, on 10th March 1858 Dr. James Pattison Walker, Jail Superintendent arrived at Port Blair with four European officers and 773 convicts to establish second penal settlement (As on 16 June 1858, out of 773 convicts 64 died in hospital, 140 escaped presumed dead, 01 committed suicide and 87 hanged). The modern history of Andaman and Nicobar Islands begins with the bringing in of 200 mutineers of 1857 mutiny in January, 1858. The second groups of political prisoners to Andamans consisted of Wahabi Convicts. Quite a large number of convicts from tharawadda who revolted against the British were also kept in Andaman. But these were all before building the Cellular Jail (present National Memorial). On May 13 when aborigines drove the absconded 81 convicts back to Port Blair Dr. J.P.Walker, the jail superintendent hanged them all in a day. Narain, convict No 61 on the 4th day of his arrival in the settlement (13-03-1858) escaped from the settlement and he was the first escaped convict. He escaped from Chatham by swimming but finally captured. After fourth day of this incidence Naringun Singh convict No 46 committed suicide. This was the first recorded suicide in the settlement. In the same month on 23-03-1858 eleven convicts escaped from the Ross Island. The convicts Schoolmuch Convict No 836, Pandoo (762), Kuttbeg (781) and Krishna Chauhan (834) on 06-04-1859 and many others tried to escape from time to time, but most of them eitther caught by the rulers or killed by the Andaman aborigines. The Viper Island was occupied on 8 Octobar 1858. The island was named after the vessel 'VIPER' which left Calcutta for Andamans with Archibald Blair on 20-12-1788. The jail in the Viper island was completed in 1867 with the purpose to give more strong caging to the convicts. The adjacent areas were that time occupied by the ferocious aborigines. Hundreds of chain-gang inmates housed in the Viper Jail. Maharaja Gajapati Bir Kishore Singh Dev, King of Jagannath Puri, Orissa was also imprisoned in Viper. He died very soon and was cremated at Dundas Point. One of the convicts I should essentially mention about. Bunnoo, a Punjabi female convict (No 4122) arrived from Karachi in April 1960. She was the bride in the first convict marriage which took place in the settlement itself. After the marriage she escaped from the Viper Island on 18-01-1861 along with her convict husband. But two days later both the bodies were found dead at sea near the Viper Island. The convicts were never treated as human beings in the rulers' camps. Evidently the prisoners were also kept as human samples under some secret pharmaceutical trials. The construction of the Cellular Jail was taken up in the year 1896 on the basis of Order No. 423 dated 13th September, 1893 issued by the then Administration. This order was issued by Col. N.M. Horsford, Superintendent of Port Blair. The

Cellular Jail was designed on the model of Pentonville prison, the first modern prison in London opened in 1816. The construction of Cellular Jail was completed in 1906, when Sir Richard Temple was the Chief Commissioner. The mode of imprisonment was notoriously called 'Kala Pani'. Now in the Cellular Jail (declared 'National Memorial' in 1979) one can see the old materials, descriptions, models and photographs exhibiting and explaining the forms of inhuman torture of those days such as flogging on triangular iron frame, bar fetters, cross bar fetters, neck, ring shackle, leg iron chains, gang chains, gunny bag uniform, oil grinding, dirty diets, coconut coir rope making, hanging by the leg in the sun, merciless beating and what not. Few of the prisoners had murdered the British officers and few like Indu Bhushan Roy (1912) and Pt Ram Rakha (1919) died in protest of the inhuman torturing of the Britishers. The earthquake of 1941 and the Japanese invasion followed by occupation of this territory by them caused substantial damage to the Jail building resulting in the demolition of 4 out of its 7 wings. When the island fell into the hands of Japanese from 23rd March, 1942 to 7th October, 1945, the prisoners and other suspected citizens were thrown under their barbarous inhuman methods. Many of them had been shot dead and many were buried in common graves. The "Humphrey Gunj Martyrs Memorial" about 15 kms from Port Blair today stands as a mute witness to the inhuman treatment meted out to the elite of Andaman by the Japanese on mere ground of suspicion. The Cellular Jail of national and historical importance was converted into a National Memorial by the then Prime Minister Shri Morarji Desai on 11th February, 1979. I really wonder that how those people who struggled, suffered and sacrificed with the patriotic spirits but built Andamans- the Quintessence of Indian culture with their glorious history are being forgotten. Now how many people do know about Sher Ali, Pandit Ramrakha, Indubhushan Roy, Narain, Allama Fazal-Haq-Khairabadi, Dr. Diwan

Singh Kalepani, Zulfiquar Ali, Musai Singh, Seetaramaraju and many other sung and unsung heroes of our freedom struggle? How many people do know about the Battle of Aberdeen? And how many people pay obeisance in their memory in the manner those great people deserve. I am sure to find very few hands up in YES.

When the second penal settlement was established, the adjoining area was populated by the Aka-bea tribes comprising of their groups Aryoto (Shore dwellers), adazig (Creek dwellers) and Eremtaga (Forest dwellers). The Jarawas were not directly affected by the establishment of penal settlements at the initial stage. There were frequent incidents of fighting between the Andamanese and the population of the settlement area. The most horrible and memorable fight was the Battle of Aberdeen. But before the battle of Aberdeen there were previously two major attacks made by the Great Andamanese. The first battle by 200 Great Andamanese was organized on 6th April 1859 in which four convict workers were killed (Portman, 1899(1):276).The second attack was made on 14th April 1859, in which 1500 Great Andamanese attacked the penal settlement killing 3 and took away some convicts with fetter on as "Prisoners of war",about whom nothing is known thereafter (Portman, 1899(1):277-8). The third attack which known as "Battle of Aberdeen", took place on 17th May 1859. Every year on 17th May, the 'Andaman Day' is observed at Port Blair to remember the valour and gallantry shown by the Andamanese tribes in their non-stop fights against the Britishers in which the major fight was fought on 17 May 1859 called to be the great 'Battle of Aberdeen'. Comparing to the battle of Aberdeen which was fought in the city of Aberdeen, Scotland on 13 September 1644 in which 160 people died, this Great Battle of Aberdeen fought in the Andaman is the deadliest one.

Let me mention what is the history behind the great Battle of Aberdeen. The Great Andamanese had their major encounter with the Britishers in 1789 AD when Lieutenant Archibald Blair arrived at Chatham Island (also named as MARK ISLAND) along with his party on basis of the report submitted to East India Company by Col. Colebrook and Captain Blair. The first penal settlement was established in 1789 at Port Blair. Col Syme who was sent on a mission to Ava in 1795, visited the establishment on his voyage out and found there a population of 700 including a company of sepoys. He estimated the aborigines at 2000 to 2500 and gave a very unflattering description of them. They then used rafts of bamboo in addition to canoes. Some estimated the aborigines were above 5000.

The new settlement was so unhealthy and fearful that it was finally decided to be abandoned in 1796. Again, in 1855 measures were proposed at Calcutta (now Kolkata) and then Dr. Federic J Mouat was sent as head of a commission to examine the islands and select a suitable locality for the establishment of second penal settlement. The commission spent few weeks and finally selected an harbour to which they gave the name of Port Blair in honour of its former resident. This expedition had several serious conflicts with the aborigines in which many tribals were killed.

On return of the commission to Calcutta their advice was soon acted on and the Late General (then Captain) H.Man was sent to Port Blair to formally re-annex the Andamans. In 1858, Dr. J.P.Walker, Jail Superintendent arrived at Port Blair with four European officers and convicts. They cleared Chatham, Ross Island, Haddo and Atlanta Point areas. The convict settlement grew up at South Point, Atlanta Point, Haddo, Junglighat and Hopetown etc. All these activities were of course towards the well planned British establishment which the Andaman natives disliked. Their true love for their motherland enforced them to come in attack against the Britishers with their simple bows and arrows. Several skirmishes took place between the aborigines and the Britishers, in most of which the aborigines had to drop the much blood and tears. But their unforgettable valour and gallantry were recognized by the Britishers too. Interestingly the Åka-bea group of the Great Andamanese were joined by many other territorial groups in their communal attacks against the colonists. The Great Andamanese had many territorial groups from south Andaman to Diglipur in north such as Jeru, Kari, Kora, Bo, Bea, Balawa, Kede, Kol, Juwai and Puckiwar.

On April 23rd ,1858 two convicts namely Doodhnath Tiwari and Sadloo with 90 other convicts escaped from the British imprisonment. The remaining convicts except Doodhnath Tiwari and Sadloo were killed by the aborigines. Surprisingly the tribals not only left Doodhnath Tiwari but allowed him to stay with them. Doodhnath Tiwari lived with them for a year and 24 days. Gradually Shri Dudhnath Tiwari became capable to understand the Andamanese language. During May 1859 Shri.Doodhnath Tiwari came to know about a communal plan of a great attack on the British camps made by the Great Andamanese. Quietly slipping away from the encampment of the aborigines in the night with Shri.Sadloo (who was staying with other group of the Great Andamanese and came in contact with the Tiwari group) Shri Doodhnath Tiwari somehow reached PortBair and informed the then Superintendent of the convict settlement about the intention of the aborigines. As result in the fight the British members were armed with modern weapons and had secured positions. None of the Britishers was wounded seriously while thousands of the tribals were shot down and seriously wounded. But the acts of bravery to protect their territory shown by the Great Andamanese deserve to receive a salutary respect from the people of free India.

It is interesting to note that in December 1866 Doodhnath Tiwari ex-convict No.276 who had escaped to the jungle in April 1858 and had lived a year with the Great Andamanese, revisited PortBlair while in the service of Major Wraughton, Assistant Commissary General who stopped at PortBlair in the vessel Arracan on his way from Calcutta to Rangoon. Homfray, Superintendent of the settlement, took Doodhnath to the Andaman Home and he was at once recognised by the Andamanese, and some of the men appeared glad to see him, though the women abused him for leaving them and especially for abandoning his wife when she was pregnant. During his stay with the aborigines he married with an Andamanese girl namely LIPA. Homfray took the opportunity of his presence in the settlement to test the accuracy of Doodhnath's statements to Dr.Walker regarding his wanderings and found them to be fairly accurate.

Meanwhile at the time when Doodhnath was camped with the aborigines and before the Battle of Aberdeen was fought, the natives had organised their attacks on two recorded occasions viz 06-04-1859 and on 14-04-1859. On 06-04-1859 when 248 convicts were engaged in their work at Haddo near Chatham Island. About 200 aborigines armed with their bows and arrows attacked and killed convicts Kuramat Khan (No 245), Baboo (No 850) and Nand Singh (No 2155). The injured Dukhram Singh (No 969) died on the next day. The other wounded convicts were Bishun Nath (No 38), E.etoo (No 790), Gangadhur Singh (No 657), Ram Singh (No 1368) and Lall Ram Latun. On 14-04-1859 about 1500 aborigines suddenly attacked and killed Bukun Singh (No 1493), Punchum Singh (No 1597) and Mohan Singh (No 1125). Among the wounded convicts were Ramlall (No 1142), Jugmohan (No 1917), Sheikh Bodun (No 694), Shougoolam (No 1919), Bhoput (No 1915) and Shoudeen (No 1763). From this attack the natives took with them 11 convicts viz. Toolea (No 1407), Dhoolee Rae (No 1119),

Nukapa (No 1403), Jan Mohammed (No 1401), Amir Ulla Khan (1756), Mookund (No 1076), Dookey (No 1086), Seebul Peerhand (No 1837), Bihari Misser (No 1603), Leedhoos (No 989), and Gajadhar (No 856). Nobody was found thereafter. We need to confirm whether at the time when the aborigines made attacks on the settlement, Doodhnath was camped with the aborigines or already left their camp. And it was also not confirmed whether the same group attacked who saved Doodhnath earlier. It is worthy to note that within less than a year after the Battle of Aberdeen, on 27-02-1860 Dr. Gamack was shown the first signs of friendship from a group of aborigines on the Chatham Island.

To refuge the aborigines when captured for various purposes the 'Andaman Home' was founded after the second penal settlement in the islands. It was founded under a policy formulated by Col.J.C.Houghton during the administration of Col. R. C. Tytler in 1862-63. There were many British Officers appointed as Officers in Charge of the Andamanese tribes. These officers were H.F. Corbyn (1863 -64), J.N. Homfray, F.E. Tuson, E.H. Man, M.V. Portman, P. Vaux, C.G. Rogers and M.C.C. Bonington (1903-05 and took the charges again in 1931).

In the Andaman Home the first Andamanese child was born in 1866. In May 1866 J.N.Homfray moved the Andaman Home from Ross Island to Port Mouat. In May 1873 at Shoal Bay Home an Andamanese woman gave birth to twins, a most unusual occurrence. Both the babies died soon after their births. The available document also mentions about the Andaman Home on Viper Island in 1875. The Andaman Home was moved from Viper to Haddo on 28-05-1882. In the month of December 1867, 80 members of the 'Kol' tribe were brought into the Andaman Home for the first time. Apart from it on 09-02-1869 a special Andamanese hospital was opened at Port Mouat. An Andamanese orphanage was also established to take care of the Andamanese children. In 1874, eleven boys escaped from the orphanage and then the rulers had to move the orphanage from the Ross Island to Viper Island. With the advent of the Japanese in 1942 the practice of the Andaman Home or Andamanese Home discontinued. During the period when 'Andaman Home' started to function, the Great Andamanese residing in the dense forests of the Great Andamans were never ready to come in friendly contact with the outsiders. The British India government made all efforts to establish friendly relationship with the island aborigines. With this objective in hand, there were many attempts made to capture the tribal members and kept them in 'Andaman Home'. In most of the cases of capture and keeping the tribes in captivity in home either the tribes died of sickness or they just sickened and had therefore to be released. The 'Andaman Home' was founded by the Britishers at Port Blair as an inn for the tribals. With the foundation of 'Andaman Home' the founders planned to convey their message of peace and friendship through Home but later adverse incidents made the British intention dubious. A sailor, Mr. Pratt tried to rape a Great Andamanese woman on 28th January 1863 and the Great Andamanese male members murdered him. Two of them were arrested and kept in detention. Few Andamanese members came to see their men who were kept in detention were forcibly kept in 'Andaman Home'. On most of the occasions, in the 'Andaman Home' the aborigines were treated as guests and they were provided with gift items and medical treatment. But ultimately the Home turned into an institution of tribal damage. The British contacts made the aborigines addicted to opium, tobacco, and liquor. The Home contributed to the spread of several diseases among the Andamanese because housing conditions were cramped and unsanitary. In one case the islanders were housed in a cattle shed, along with the cattle (Portman 1899: 477- 478). The first reported epidemic in 1868, five years after the opening of the 'Andaman Home', involved bronchial pulmonary infections. From 1864 to 1870, the Britishers reported 150 births in the Home; but of these children not one lived beyond two years (Census of India 1911: 78). In spite of the fact that the Andamanese were befriended by the Britishers in the Andaman Homes, all of the tribes were not in the hands of the Britishers. On 06-05-1876 two persons involved in collection of swiflet birds' nests were killed by the natives. In 1877-78, twelve escaped convicts had been captured by the Andamanese. In February 1875, Man noticed syphilitic sores on some Andamanese staying at the 'Andaman Home' on Viper Island. Investigations revealed that these islanders had been suffering from the disease for some four years. Purportedly the interim charge of the Andamanese noticed sores in January of 1875, but nothing was done to prevent its spread. Portman opined that the disease had probably been in existence for six years. A convict working at the Viper Island was blamed for spreading the disease after he raped Andamanese women (Portman 1899, Vol. 2:597-607). Man tried to isolate those Andamanese infected with the disease, but they resisted being confined in the hospital and fled to the forest. As per the adimistrative report of 1880-81, 98 Andamanese suffering from Syphilis were admitted in the hospital. At the time when syphilis had been detected at the Home, it was found that all of the tribes in south and middle Andaman also were infected with the disease. Reportedly, opthalmia (an eye infection) broke out leaving many islanders partially or completely blind. Man himself became infected with this illness (Mathur 1984:168).

In the 'Andaman Home' the tribes were decimated by a series of epidemics e.g. Pneumonia (1868), Syphilis (1876), Measles (1877), Influenza (1892). As result the Andamanese population rapidly dwindled down.

Being the first of its kind in the history of the Andaman tribes, an Andamanese was officially executed on 19-05-1880 for killing three persons. The Andamanese namely Bialola S/o Wologa Jola, the chief of the Port Mouat Sept on 24-07-

1878 killed a girl of the same sept. He killed another girl, daughter of a Hindu convict and an Andamanese woman on 31-07-1878. The only reason for these murders was that Bialola had been disturbed in his sleep by the children. In September 1878, the Chief Commissioner sentenced him to two years rigorous imprisonment. In February 1880 yet another murder after his release from the Viper Jail he committed. He killed Riala by shooting arrows on his stomach. He was immediately hanged to death.

Due to some unknown reasons the Great Andamanese who became far stronger by the time of the second settlement had occupied almost the entire land around the harbour, having driven the Jarawas into the hinterland. There was frequent fighting between the two groups. The British later used the Great Andamanese as trackers and fighters during numerous punitive expeditions where shotguns were used against the Jarawa. They (Andmanese) were paid with food, tobacco, opium and alcohol and even issued with arms and ammunition. It is mentioned in the available record that in 1865 the Andamanese first began to use the dogs for pig hunting, which they learnt from the Burmese escaped convicts. In March 1867, an agriculture exhibition was organised on Ross Island with participation of many aborigines. In the same year Capt F.C. Anderson, Barrack Master of Fort William, Calcutta applied to Col. B. Ford for two Andamanese boys, who he said he was willing to adopt and educate. In November 1867 two Andamanese boys namely 'Kiddy Boy' and 'Topsy' were sent to him. The British officers continued to establish friendly relationship with the Great Andamanese with the purposes differed from time to time and case to case. In 1882, Maj. Wimberley took an Andamanese girl with him to New Zealand and soon brought her back to Port Blair where she died of illness. In 1883, few Andamanese including women were brought to Calcutta for the purpose of being modeled for an Internation Exhibition.

But all the Great Andamanese were not in the handshake distance with the British rulers (for example, on 07-10-1885 convict Petty Officer Habibi (No 25399) was murdered by some Andamanese on the east coast of the South Andaman near 'Lakera Barnga'). Despite numerous killings by the aborigines the visit of the Andamanese from the interiors to the settlement continued. In June 1889, 92 Andamanese from the Middle and North of Andamans visited the settlement (Admn Report 1889-90, p.59).

Supported by the friendly Great Andamanese there were many attempts made by the Britishers to capture the Jarawa and bring them under the British influence. The British policy of giving the captives gifts and then allowing them go free did not bring the hoped results. Their attempts at capturing Jarawa men, teaching them Hindi or English and then setting them free to function as intermediaries did not work. On some occasions Jarawa members were captured and kept under captivation for few days with purpose to befriend them, could not be achieved. The Jarawas under captivation either died of sickness or became so unhealthy that they had to be released by the rulers.

In July 1863, as is already known, Corbyn led a party to find a passage through the interior from Port Blair to the other side on the western coast. They did not come across any Jarawa as such, but two of the Andamanese, Toby and Jack gave to understand that there was a possibility of their encountering "an unfriendly tribe of aborigines of whom they themselves seemed to be in great dread". Ford, in a report written on 3 January 1865 stated that the aborigines inland on the south side were the most troublesome. It is obvious that he was referring to the Jarawas. In December 1875, the Jarawas captured six convicts and few of them were kept in captivity for about 19 days. In the following years Jarawa huts were looted, their weapons and utensils brought out on different occasions. As a sort of compensation some presents like matches, pipes, tobacco, looking glasses etc. were left in the Jarawa huts but these were unknown to the tribes. On many occasions the Jarawas were captured and brought to Port Blair and sent back after few days. Many a time in the years that followed, clashes of one kind or the other took place, because it became more and more apparent that the Jarawas distrusted every one, particularly the Great Andamanese.

In his annual report for the year 1882 – 83, Godwin-Austin (who had temporarily taken over the charges from Maurice Vidal Portman during the latter's absence on leave) wrote:

"The Jarawas have given much more trouble during the past year than hitherto." And perhaps, he surmised, this was due to the fact that "much had been done in the way of opening out tracks through their country". The Jarawas distrusted the Great Andamanese too because the Britishers used them (the Great Andamanese) as their fighters against the Jarawa. Most of the Jarawa captures have failed to gain the goal in favour of the Britishers. Portman writes in 1894 –95: "I am of the opinion that the only way to catch the Jarawas will be by sending out armed parties of police and convicts, as was done on former occasion when they were caught and using our Andamanese merely as trackers as they are too afraid of the Jarawas to make any real effort to catch them when alone and unsupported by firearms".

The North Sentinel Island is presently inhabited by Sentinelese but as per the historical statements of British officers, the Island was inhabited by the Jarawa. May be the present island tribes (Sentinelese) are actually Jarawa or the present Sentinelese were discovered to be the Jarawa by the Britishers by mistake. In March 1867, Humphrey writes:

"I had occasion. In pursuit of runaways, to visit the North Sentinel Island, a distance of about 25 miles to the Westward of Port Mout with some Great Andamanese accompanying me. We saw some ten men on the beach, naked, long haired and with bows and arrows shooting fish. My friends told me that they were Jurrah wallahs (Jarawa men) who were not friendly to them, having some years past encountered some of the tribe on Rutland Island in which their chief was wounded."

The North Sentinel Island was left alone for centuries and for the first time in history Portman and Cadell landed on the island in 1880. In his second visit in the same year Portman was able to capture a woman and four small children and the tribes were released soon.

Portman as obvious from his report in 1894 had felt that the Jarawas on North Sentinel Island (?) could be tamed for scientific and other reasons. "Portman suggested a small policy as far as the Jarawas on Rutland Island was concerned. But there is nothing on record to show whether or not the policy or the methods suggested by him were taken into effect. However, the fact remains that the so-addressed Jarawas of North Sentinel Island were always unfriendly to them.

In 1870 during the rule of Lord Mayo many convicts were given freedom of movement and were encouraged to marry convict women with the idea of settling them and expanding agriculture in the islands. With the increase in number of convict population agriculture was encouraged in the islands. By the end of the year 1894-95 an area of 22,306 acres were cleared and 10,140 acres of land were cultivated in which 4,425 acres of land was bearing tea, coffee, cocoa, coconuts and vegetables. The island population was steadily increasing from 14,628 in 1881(11,440 in Port Blair). In 1883 the Forest Department was established. After its establishment, the Department of Forest planted large number of pterocarpus dalbergioides (Padauk) which and exotics like eucalyptus have caused extensive ecological damage to the native forests.

The exploitation of timber from the forest was already taking place since the formation of the penal colony in these islands. A saw mill recognized as one of the biggest saw mills in Asia was established on Chatham Island connected with Port Blair with help of a long wooden bridge. This bridge on which we children would come for fishing with lines and hooks is now replaced by a cemented bridge.

When on 25th March 1884, a Jarawa group was sighted; a fight with bows and arrows ensued. One Jarawa man was killed and another got injury in his leg. The wounded Jarawa namely Talai was taken to Port Blair. After his recovery Talai had a friendly term with Mr. Portman, Officer-in-charge of the Andamanese. With a great hope and enthusiasm with Talai, 30 convicts and a large number of Andmanese, Mr. Portman led an expedition to contact the Jarawas but all his hopes crushed when Talai quietly absconded himself and disappeard. Then the British attempts to capture the Jarawas, teach them and get them free to play role of intermediary did not work. Later on another Jarawa boy was caught and the Talai case repeated.

On a most interesting odd incident I must narrate—two Jarawas were captured on 7th April, 1885 by the Britishers with the help of Great Andamanese and victims. One captured Jarawa woman fell in love with one Great Andamanese boy namely Mark and she wanted him to go with her. Mark did not give any active response to her. This is a rare case of love between Jarawa and Great Andamanese.

Portman, after he got success in befriending the Onge tribe on Little Andaman in 1886 was hoping to repeat it with the Jarawa, especially since he thought them to be closely related to the Onge. But it did not work. Because of more forests were being cleared and more encroachments into the tribal territory being noticed, the Jarawas became more unfriendly even after 1901. In the years around 1901-02, the punitive expeditions of the Britishers were conducted mainly in the areas of Jatang Hill (a survey station of that period), Port Meadows, Pochang, around Napier Bay and Petman Island etc and near Bilap Bay on the west.

Again in 1901, another punitive expedition headed by Fawcett who was in military command was conducted but failed. Such expeditions lasted from 1901 to 1920 and onwards. But significantly nothing in favour of the Britishers was gained. Not a single Jarawa was captured.

On 24th February in 1902 a team of Gilbert Rogers, the Deputy Conservator of Forests, Bonig, Assistant Harbour Master, Messrs Vaux, one policeman, three convicts and sixteen Great Andamanese was sent by Sir Richard Temple, the then Chief Commissioner on a punitive expedition against the Jarawa. In this expedition in the fight Mr. Vaux was died of attack by the Jarawas. Mr. Vaux was an active officer working under the Chief Commissioner. He was a fond of manhunt as he proved himself in previous punitive expeditions among the Jarawas. That time the logging operations were progressive with help of elephants, the cellular Jail was under construction, and there were some brickfields at Port Blair. Col. Temple appointed Mr. Vaux as team leader of the punitive expedition. They had a boat with them named 'Belle'. On 18 February, they made a sudden attack on some sleeping Jarawas. As result how many natives died not known but a woman, two children and a motherless infant came into their captivity. Again on 24th February in the moonlight they entered a Jarawa camp to capture the Jarawas. In this attack the Jarawas ran out of their hut but not far away. They targeted Mr. Vaux in light of their hearth and shot arrows which did not fail. Mr. Vaux died on the spot. Thus he paid the price for his disloyal attack on the tribes who were simply living in their own abode. In the later part of the period all the British efforts to capture the Jarawa and to befriend them went in vain to greater extent. The

Jarawa raids became so daring that in 1917 a train on a tram line was held up.

On 26th Feb, 1918, another punitive expedition was organized by D.L. Morgan and his team consisted of 12 Great Andamanese,16 policemen and 35 convicts. They had an encounter with the Jarawas but the expedition went fruitless. One more expedition was conducted by C.G. Fields accompanied by Baines, 15 policemen, 6 Great Andamanese and 40 convicts on 8th March 1921. This expedition also had been vain. In another punitive expedition in 1925 many Jarawas were killed by the Britishers. Thus the Britishers' all efforts to capture and befriend the natives did not fetch expected result. The natives were untamed purely.

In 1929 a Swedish multinational Wimco commenced a match splint factory at Port Blair near Chatham. The company joined the already working Chatham Saw Mill to accelerate the process of deforestation in the islands. Further three major industries namely Asian Polymers Pvt Ltd, Jaishree Timber Products and a Plywood making company namely Andaman Timber Industries with many wood based factories started working which resulted in massive deforestation in the islands. Despite the Jarawa attacks against logging operations, the forest clearance for expansion and development of the settlements was continued. The demand for wood for fulfilling the requirements of the sawmills, WIMCO match splint factory, ATI plywood manufacturing factory at Bambooflat and other small scale industries were increasing day by day. During that period the people were arriving by two ships viz. S.S.Maharaja and S.S. Shahjahan to Port Blair from Rangoon, Madras (now Chennai) and Calcutta (now Kolkata). These two ships plied regularly between these places. The population was also increasing. The great fire incident in the WIMCO factory is still vivid in my memory.

Towards the end of the 19th century, Jarawa raiding activities increased considerably. MYKA wrote: Finally, there is a proposal to the colonial government by the then Chief Commissioner Cosgrave of 1938 to deport all Andamanese to an uninhabited island but it was then rejected. The official reply stated, "The Jarawas are the original inhabitants of the island and we have some obligation not to interfere with the occupation of their ancient habitat more than they themselves make it necessary." Cosgrave was also advised to keep the Jarawa at a distance as much as possible.

The Jarawa raids continued even after India attained Independence and British left the islands forever. Their obstinate and aggressive hostility together with their refusal to allow any contact caused some highly specific problems to the settler population and government. The reasons for the past failed attempts in befriending the Jarawa became a much-discussed subject for decades. An expansion of settlements into the Jarawa territory has been one of the main problems. The bombings during the Japanese occupation towards the end of World War II have also been considered as one reason.

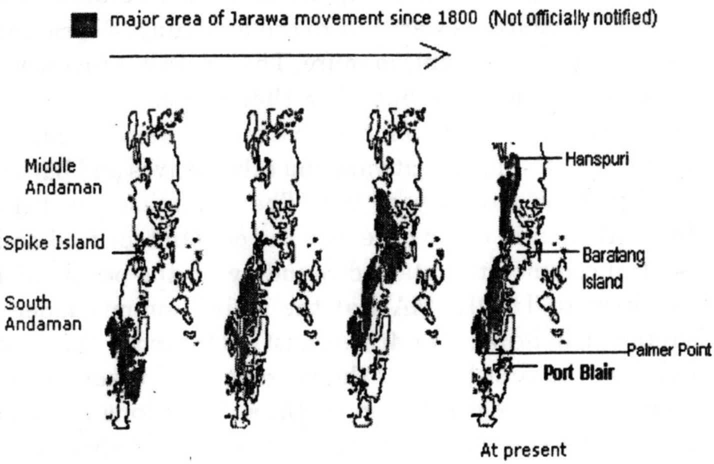

During the World War II, Japanese troops occupied the islands between 23rd March 1942 and 7th October 1945. The Jarawa territory was bombed and the movement by Jarawa groups towards the north in the direction of Middle Great Andaman was observed. During the Regime of the Japanese, the Jarawas were not only the group to live in terror. The general people were also nervous and scared of the inhuman tortures of the Japanese. On 30-03-1943, few citizens of Port Blair were killed at Dignabad Hill by the Japanese under spy case. On 19-10-1943, about 300 citizens of Port Blair were arrested by the Japanese. After three days on 23-10-1943 Dr. Diwan Singh, a local doctor with all the active members of the Indian Independence League, the Peace Committee and the Punjabi Literary Society was arrested by the Japanese at Port Blair. On 30-01-1944, under spy case 44 citizens of Port Blair were shot down at Homfray Gunj by the Japanese. During the Japanese period the islanders witnessed unforgettable inhuman treatment and mass killings of the innocent people. As per an available description, there was acute shortage of food. The Japanese soldiers suffered also badly. The local people were put to hard work to raise sweet potato, tapioca and other edible crops. The local inhabitants were put to the ignominy of spraying human excreta as organic manure. They were producing for the Japanese soldiers but they themselves were going hungry. Clothes had become a luxury. People used gunny bags for clothes, had to eat yam and other leaves and barks. There was no sanctity of life. The Japanese military administration in order to reduce the demand for food and essential commodities started rounding up the people and took them to THOKUMAN at the Chief Commissioner's secretariat building. On 4th August 1945 under the first round up, the first batch of the persons were taken to the uninhabited Havelock Island by three boats (one of them named 'AKBAR'). On reaching near the island they were forced to jump into the sea, in which many of them died and few of them survived in forest of the island. One of the survivors was Saudagar. In his struggle to survive he ate human flesh of his dead compatriots. He was rescued in October 1945 by a British war ship 'Narbada'. The officer who saved him was Lt. Taylor. During my college days I often saw this old man on our college road. The present Jawaharlal Nehru Rajkeeya Mahavidhyala at Port Blair was then named as the 'Government College'. That time I did not know about his history but he was in our constant watch for his lope on the college road at this so old age. We saw him always with a stick abnormally waving in the air from his shoulder to the earth while walking. The second round up was carried in Garacharma village. The old and infirm unemployed persons were taken to Tetlyers' Ghat in Port Mouat. Nobody returned back from there and nothing is still known about them. The third round up was prepared but before the final operation the Japanese had to leave the island. On the other hand the Nicobarese tribes were no less sufferers; they also faced the volley of cruelties and barbarisms committed on them by the Japanese. Many of them were tortured to death. Such was the scene in the islands at that time. The Japanese destroyed all records when they left. The principal sources are an unpublished report by local resident Rama Krishna: *The Andaman Islands under Japanese Occupation 1942-5*, another unpublished account by a British Officer, D. McCarthy: *The Andaman Interlude* (he was sent on a secret mission to the islands in 1944), together with the memories of the older inhabitants interviewed by historians. All these, and the published works which draw upon them, are in agreement that the occupation saw numerous atrocities committed by the Japanese against the local population. On 07-10-1945, with the re-occupation, the military administration ended. The civil administration was started by Patterson Neol Kennedy, ICS and he was the first and the last British Chief Commissioner of the Andaman and Nicobar Islands. After the Britishers regained the islands the efforts to capture the natives continued. On the other hand the settler population had come down from about 21000 to just around 14000 after the penal settlement was dismantled after the British reoccupation. Those who wished to go back to their home towns were permitted to go. About 4000 people had left the island and over 3000 were massacred by the Japanese.

Some recorded major events of the British Period concerning the Jarawas

1863 : In July 1863, Carbyn led a party to find a passage through the interior from Port Blair to the other side on the western coast. They did not come across any Jarawa as such, but two of the Andamanese, Topby and Jacko gave Carbyn to understand that there was a possibility of their encountering "an unfriendly tribe of aborigines of whom they themselves seemed to be in great dread". Ford, in a report written on 3 January 1865 stated that the aborigines inland on the south side were the most troublesome. "It is obvious that he was referring to the Jarawas.

1872 : The first Jarawa raid on settlement took place during the year. Further clothes and tools of the convicts were also robbed (Admn. Report 1871-72, pg 49).

1875 : Four convicts were killed by the Jarawas on Kyd Island. (One convict was killed and two were captured, all runaways) (1901 Census, pg 68).

1875 : An expedition was organized by Goodur, a convict zamadaar during the period of D.M.Stewart, Chief Commissioner. In the punitive expedtion two Jarawas (one pregnant woman and an old man) were captured and six convicts were killed.

1875: In December 1875, the Jarawas captured six convicts and few of them were kept in captivity for about 19 days. In the following years Jarawa huts were looted, their weapons and utensils brought out on different occasions. As a sort of compensation some presents like matches, pipes, tobacco, looking glasses etc. were left in the Jarawa huts but these were unknown to the tribes.

1876-77: Many expeditions were conducted during this period.

1878 : The Jarawas attacked on the Brigade Creek, Andamanese Home and one man was killed (Portman, pg 720). In an expedition one woman and two children were caught by the Britishers at Constance Bay.

1879 : Nine Jarawas were captured but the Britishers had to release them.

1880 : In a conflict with Aka-bea tribes of the Great Andamanese, an Andamanese man was killed by the Jarawas at the Tarachang home at Port Campbell (Portman 1899, Vol. II:729).

1882 : Andamanese skirmish with Jarawa at Goplakabang, but friendly signs at Kalatang (A&N manual 1886, pg 284). But in the same year in an attack four convicts were killed by the Jarawas.

1883 : Jarawa attacked on the settlement. Five convicts were killed at Rangachang. One Jarawa woman was captured (1901 Census, pg 68).

1884 : On 25th March 1884, a Jarawa group was sighted; a fight with bows and arrows ensued. One Jarawa man was killed and another got injury in his leg. The wounded Jarawa namely Talai was taken to Port Blair. After his recovery Talai had a friendly term with Mr. Portman, Officer-in-charge of the Andamanese. In another Jarawa attack a police constable was wounded at Miletilak. One Jarawa was killed, two captured (one wounded).At Rangachang four Jarawa women and one man were captured and released. Jarawa hut found in the Jarawa Khari Valley (1901 Census, pg 68).

1885 : A Jarawa raid on the settlement at Ograbraj, 2 Jarawa women captured and released(1901 Census, pg 68).

1887 : A Jarawa raid on the settlement took place. Andamanese camp at Chaual (Northwest corner of South Andaman) was attacked in which one boy wounded (F.Admn.Report, 913-14, pg 8).

1888 : Jarawa raid occurred in the settlement. One convict was killed and one escaped at Tusnabad and one killed at Mathura. Convict boat attacked at Tytler's Ghat in Port Mouat (P.Lall, pg 67).

1889 : Jarawa attacked on the settlement. Andamanese camp at Port Mouat attacked. One man wounded (1908 Gazetteer, pg 10).

1890 : Jarawa attack on the Andamanese camp at Port Campbell in which one man wounded and one Jarawa child captured. The captured female child was adopted by an Andamanese woman. Unfortunately she fell ill and died in hospital in August 1891.

1890 : On 10-11-1890 three self supporting convicts of Kadakachang village were murdered by the Jarawas.

1891 : Jarawa attacked on a settlement and one convict at Brindaban was wounded.

1892 : Jarawa raid on the settlement occurred. Andamanese camp at Bajajag was attacked in which one girl was killed.

1893 : Jarawa attacked on an Andamanese settlement near Homfray's Strait. One man was killed while one was injured.

1894 : Jarawa raid on the settlement occurred. An Andamanese who was hunting a turtle was killed at Port Mouat.

1895 : Jarawa raid on the settlement occurred at Cadellgunj. 2 convicts at Cadellgunj and 2 more convicts at Rutland Island in other attack were killed. Capturing of Jarawas were also made but soon they had to be released.

1896 : In a Jarawa attack on the Great Andamanese settlement, one Jarawa was wounded at Bluff Island. Further the Jarawas attacked on an Andamanese camp at Goplakabang. A Jarawa community hut was also discovered at Constance Bay.

1898 : Jarawa attacked on a settlement in which 1 convict was killed at Tarachang Home. A Jarawa village was found at Torabi Hill. In another attack 3 convicts were killed at Cadellgunj.

1899 : Jarawa raid took place in the settlement. A temporary Barrack of convicts at Jirkatanag was attacked. 2 convicts, 1 friendly Andamanese and 1 Jarawa were wounded.

1901 : A punitive expedition headed by Fawcett who was in military command was conducted but failed.

1902 : On 11-01-1902 the Jarawas attacked the Forest department where the convicts were engaged in their works at Jatang and 2 convicts were killed. Some women and children were captured and they were brought to Port Blair and after a few days they were taken back to their forest. On February 24 Mr. Vaux, a British officer was killed by the Jarawas during a punitive expedition.

1905 : The 'Bush Police' was established in the settlement involving few selected friendly Great Andamanese with a Burmese as their head.

1914 : As per the Chief Commissioner's Notification No.6, Middle Strait (23411 acres), the Port Meadows (12160 acres) and Shoal Bay (9728 acres) were declared as Reserve Forests, which was a Jarawa area(Forest Admn Report 1913-14, p.10).

1918 : A punitive expedition was organized on 26th February, 1918, by D.L. Morgan and his team consisted of 12 Great Andamanese, 16 Policemen and 35 convicts. They had an encounter with the Jarawas but the expedition went fruitless.

1921 : An expedition was conducted by C.G. Fields accompanied by Baines, 15 policemen, 6 Great Andamanese and 40 convicts on 8th March 1921. This expedition also had been failed to gain the goal.

1925 : In a punitive expedition many Jarawas were killed by the Britishers.

1946 : On 13-11-1946 near Miletilak Creek an elephant was found dead with 26 arrows in its body.

2

The Policies and Attitudes of the Rulers

Prior to Independence the British and Japanese policy of isolation left the tribals to themselves and almost no efforts were made to develop them except some efforts to contact and befriend them mainly for peaceful colonization and administration.

Fights were frequent between the colonists and the natives in which thousands of the innocent tribe were killed. Through the fights and punitive expeditions many forests dwellers were captured and kept in detention for days and months for various and dubious reasons. Many women were raped and tortured. Only few of the cases were recorded. Gradually the Great Andamanese and the Onges were befriended while the Jarawas and the Sentinelese remained untamed. The Britishers started using the friendly Great Andamanese members in fights against the Jarawas and Onges. Bombs were dropped on the land occupied by the Jarawa.

During the initial period of occupation, the British cleared a large portion of the forest. This led to the tribes to go back far away from the colonies, leaving the territory, which they considered of their own. In 1870, during the rule of Lord Mayo, many convicts were given freedom of movement and were encouraged to marry convict women with the idea of settling them and expanding agriculture in the islands. With increase in the number of convict population, requirement of food naturally rose and the local production of vegetables and other food items needed an immediate expansion. Under these circumstances agriculture was encouraged in the islands. On the other hand the exploitation of timber from the forest was already taking place since the formation of penal colony in these islands. The plight of the tribal communities was further aggravated by the enunciation and implementation of the National Forest Policy in 1894 by the British, which curbed the traditional rights of the tribals in forest. The efforts were also made to take the aboriginals to the mainland and other parts. But few proposals which were predicted to harm the tribals failed in obtaining the consent of the persons like Mauvat, Haughton, Corbyn, Homfray, Man and Portman.

Elwin (1939) supported the establishment of sort of 'National Park' of the tribals and advised that their contact with outside world should be reduced to the minimum. Again in 1941 he supported the idea of 'isolationism' to a great extent.

The tribal communities were brutally dealt with at the time of British and Japanese occupation and the conflict continued to be bloody even after the Independence. Unfortunately in free India in 1953 the islands' the then Chief Commissioner requested in all seriousness that a sea plane be provided to enable the islands' administration to bomb the Jarawa camps who attacked the settlers. But the god blessed the innocent natives. The request was finally rejected.

After India gained Independence, Pt. Jawaharlal Nehru, the first Prime Minister of Free India suggested that the approach should be to develop the 'synthesis' or 'integration' without destroying the rare and precious values of the tribal people.

Pt. Jawaharlal Nehru laid down five fundamental principles, which are known as 'Tribal Panchsheel':

1. People should develop alongwith the time of their own genius and we should avoid imposing anything on them. We should try to encourage in everything their own traditional art and culture.
2. Tribal rights in land and forest should be respected.
3. We should try to train and build up a team of their people to do the work of administration and development. Some technical personnel from outside will no doubt be needed, especially in the beginning. But we should avoid introducing too many outsiders into tribal territory.
4. We should not over-administer these areas or overwhelm them with a multiplicity of schemes, we should rather work through and not in rivalry to, their own social and cultural institutions.
5. We should judge results not by statistics or the amount of money spent, but the quality or human character that is evolved.

In the Andaman and Nicobar Islands the Government has undertaken certain preventive, protective and progressive measures for the welfare of the Primitive Tribes. In 1956 the islands received the status of a Union Territory. In the course of registering the population, on 31st March 1959 all six tribes namely Nicobarese, Shompen, Onge, Great Andamanese, Sentinelese and the Jarawa were placed on the List of Scheduled Tribes. This act gave them constitutional protection and the right to self-determination. Under the

Andaman & Nicobar Islands (Protection of Aboriginal Tribes) Regulation, 1956 no non-tribal can enter the tribal areas without the permission of the competent authority. No one can exploit the resources, conduct trade and business or acquire tribal property without the permission of the Administrator. The poachers and the exploiters are booked and punished under this law. In addition substantial areas in the islands are demarcated 'Tribal Reserve' under Andaman & Nicobar Islands (Protection of Aboriginal Tribes) Regulation,1956.

Similar to the Britishers' many attempts the Andaman & Nicobar Administration made efforts to establish friendly relationship with the Jarawa and Sentinelese. The Andaman and Nicobar Administration launched contact expeditions periodically to befriend the Jarawas at certain contact points in Middle Andaman. During one such expedition one band of the Jarawa showed some signs of friendliness in 1968, the credit for which must be given to Shri.Bakhtawar Singh, the then superintendent of Police, who headed the Bush Police. It all started with three Jarawa boys who entered Kadamtala of Middle Andaman. They were captured by the Bush Police and brought to Port Blair. They were kept for a month and sent back with gifts. Thereafter, gift dropping in the area where they presumably lived was intensified. Let me tell in detail how it happened... In all the administrative contact expeditions the de-facto team leader was Sardar Bakhtawar Singh. He was looking like the grand old 'Santa Clause' whose life was dedicated to befriending the unpredictable Jarawas for over three decades. Late Bakhtawar Singh had a deep love for the natives. He as a young recruit joined the Andaman and Nicobar Military Police in 1935. During his later career he served in the Bush Police till 1976 and then worked as the first Executive Secretary of the Andaman Adim Janjati Vikas Samiti at Port Blair. He said in detail that during the construction of the Andaman Trunk Road in 1968, some settlers near Kadamtala sat in ambush during the night to catch the culprit who was stealing their bananas. Three grown up Jarawa boys unaware of the trap were caught by the settlers who after initial bashing up during the night, handed them over to Kadamtala Bush Police. These natives were brought to Port Blair and kept in Cellular Jail for a month or so. They were looked after well with due care and compassion, and later released in the forest of Middle Andaman with plenty of bananas and coconuts. It was during this period that Bakhtawar Singh and his team workers could see that the natives have some preference for red colour. The period 1968-74 saw some contact efforts which brought Jarawas face- to- face with occasional contact parties, but they did not come within hand shake distance. On the other hand the Jarawas of south Andaman were constantly compelled to continue their attacks on the workers engaged in road construction and timber extraction. The construction of the present ATR started in 1973. But when the severe attacks of the natives frequented the work of construction was finally handed over to the Border Road Organisation (BRO) who used to erect fence around the site with the electric wires to be charged in nights. Several Jarawas were electrocuted and died. Few forest camps and timber depots were also established at Putatang, Punanallah, Middle Strait, Kotara, Bamboo Tikrey and Lal Tikrey. The scenario became more horrible for the Jarawas when they started grazing of elephants in their areas. The Jarawas attacked the elephants too. Fights of the natives against the increasing machinery, dogs and cattles continued.

In April 1974, in a contact expedition a few Jarawas were seen making their hut near Lakera Lungta. Seeing the approaching boat they ran away. The party members entered their hut and waited for few hours. The disappointed team returned back to their vessel. The next day they again visited the area. This time the Jarawas swam to them and scrambled for gifts. Some of them boarded their small boat.

The first organized contact trip came to Chota Ling Bang Bay on the west coast of the Middle Andaman, north of Yadita area on 11-04-1974. This was the fateful day when the noted cinematographer Prema Vaidya shot his famous film "Man in Search of Man." This film bagged the best award in the Venice Film Festival. T.N.Pandit of the Anthropological Survey of India rendered historical background for the film, while Sardar Bakhtawar Singh arranged all basic ground situations. He himself appears in the film in many shots.

Since the first successful contact established with a small Jarawa band in 1974 the Andaman and Nicobar Administration conducted periodical contact expeditions to befriend the Jarawa and to study them which has been discontinued after the Jarawas themselves in groups started coming out of forest without bows and arrows in 1997-98. The contact expedition party contacted them at Yadita, Foul Bay, Chotalingbang Bay and Lakera Lungta. In the contact expeditions the team members took with them strips of red cloths, dehusked coconuts, bananas and iron items to attract and prompt the Jarawas to come close. If you closely watch the video clips and photographs of the previous contact expeditions you can well observe that to some team members particularly the anthropologists and other experts it was an opportunity to study the tribes while to some members it was just a fun. But on the other hand the Jarawas of other groups were unfriendly towards the outsiders. They killed many of the settlers in different cases. During that period the tourists were coming in less number in the islands but the photos were abundantly available in all local studios. The cameramen who were hired or the photo unit of the contact expeditions were the main sources of the saleable Jarawas' nude and semi-nude photographs. Unfortunately on this holy land of martyrs of India's freedom struggle no photograph of a freedom fighter was available with no buyer to purchase. In a contact expedition in 1977 two Jarawa members were brought to Port Blair for few days and left at their habitat with gifts (banana)in adequate quantity. But they continued to kill the poachers. I am agree with Dr. Vishvajit Pandya, an eminent anthropologist who has rightly commented that when gift taking by a Jarawa is considered as 'their friendly gesture' in a contact expedition then why on taking something by them from the settlements is construed as their hostility? (Pandya:1999).

During the Plan period 1975-76, a Tribal Welfare Administrative Cell in the Secretariat at Port Blair was established with an Assistant Commissioner as incharge of this cell. With a view to provide special care to the primitive tribes of these islands, an autonomous organization known as Andaman Adim Janjati Vikas Samiti was founded. After its formation on 25th March'1976, Andaman Adim Janjati Vikas Samiti (AAJVS) is working with the main objectives i.e. to prevent extinction of the tribes, protect them, promote the socio-economic development of the tribes, solve the tribal problems and to develop the socio-economic environment essential to the survival and growth of the tribes. The central objective of the tribal development was their socio-economic progress with a view to integrate them with the mainstream on a footing of equality while maintaining their culture autonomy to the largest extent possible. It was also included in the tribal development strategies that there shall be a search for proper design of development which will carry their natural talent, cultural norms, value systems and personal traits with the imperatives of growth and modernization.

The welfare schemes through the plan and policy initially seemed very good but in their after effects the settlements of Great Andamanese and Onges became graveyards of their cultural deaths. Gradually the people started realizing the gaps between 'the people' and 'the papers'.

Since our present understanding of the Jarawa community was not sufficient enough to warrant any long-term policy measure, at this juncture a seminar on 'Future Policy Towards the Primitive Tribes' was organized by the AAJVS in December 1995 at Port Blair. In pursuance of the recommendations of the seminar a six month Pilot Project to have a deeper insight into the Jarawa life was launched from September 1996. The contacts with the Sentinelese were also intensified. A handbook on Jarawa language has been prepared by the Central Institute of Indian Languages, Mysore, the copies of which have been distributed among the field functionaries to bring more proficiency in their work avoiding the language barrier.

In order to augment the food resources in the Jarawa territory, schemes of dispersed plantation, sea ranching, project pig and installation of fish aggregation device have been implemented. Under the dispersed plantation seedlings to provide various kinds of fruit were planted in Jarawa Reserve. With the help of the Department of Agriculture 50 banana, 100 coconuts, 25 guava and 25 jackfruit seedlings were raised at Jarawa area during June 1999. In the same year on 15.09.1999, 25 Nos. seedlings of fruit bearing trees were raised. Later on many occasions seedlings to enrich the Jarawa reserve with food resources were planted. In the Jarawa concentrated area like Lakera Lungta and Spike Island the coconut seedlings were raised in favour of the tribes. As per another record 325 Nos. of seedlings of fruit bearing trees were planted between March'99 and August'99 at Jarawa area. Such efforts were of course assumed to be correct and then appreciated but that time actually the after impact of such activities on the ecological balance of the reserve not minded so seriously. Under the program of Sea ranching on 03.02.99 molluscs were released into the shallow water of Lakera Lungta and gillnets were distributed to the Jarawas. On 02.03.1999, 220 Nos. of molluscs were broadcasted in the creeks and fishing nets tied at R. K. Nallah and B.D Nallah and demonstrated the art of fishcatch to the Jarawa tribes. Subsequently on 14.05.1999 250 Nos. of molluscs have been released at R. K. Nallah. Apart from it fish aggregation artificial traps have been installed at Lakera Lungta area for the benefit of the Jarawa. Fishing materials like hooks, nuts etc have also been supplied to them.

Looking to the examples of the Onge and the Great Andamanese it has been realized that handling the Primitive Jarawa tribe is a sensitive and important issue and the Andaman and Nicobar Administration now is trying to tackle it with a cautious approach. What the local administration utmost conscious of is the health and hygiene of the Jarawa community. As far as the medical coverage is concerned, the Jarawa have shown considerable interest in the modern modes of treatment. The Jarawa patients were treated in GB Pant Hospital, Port Blair, Primary Health Centre Tushnabad, Primary Health Centre Kadamtala and at different Jarawa habitats like Lakera Lungta, Foul Bay and Dhaninallah etc.

There has been a long journey of the policies and approaches towards welfare of the Andaman tribes adopted by different administrators from Dr. J.P.Walker(1858-59), Captain Haughton(1859-1862), R.L.Tytler(1862-1864), Lt.Col.Ford (1864-1868), Col.H.Man (1868-1871), Major D.M.Stewart (1871-1872), Gen. Donald Martin Stewart (1872-1875), Major General C.A.Barwell (1875-1879), Col. T.Cadel (1879-1892), Col.N. Horsford (1892-94), Col. Sir Richard C.Temple (1894-1903), F.E.Tuson (1903-1904), W.R.H. Merk (1904-06), Lt.Col. H.A. Browing (1906-13), Lt.Col. M.W. Doughlas (1913-1920), Col.H.C.Beaddon (1920-1923), Lt.Col. M.L. Ferrar (1923-31), J.W.Smith (1931-1935), Sir W.A.Cosgrave (1935-1938), Sir C.E. Waterfall (1938-1942) imprisoned by the Japanese, N.K.Peterson (1945-47), I. Majid (1947-49) being the first administrator of free Andaman and Nicobar Islands, A.K.Ghosh (1949-53), S.N. Maitra (1953-56), C.Ramachandran (1956), T.G.N.Ayyar (1956-58), M.V.Rajwade (1958-61), B.N.Maheshwari (1961-65), B.L.Chak (1965-66), Mahabir Singh (1966-68), H.S.Bhutia (1968-72), Harmander Singh (1972-75), S.M.Krishnatri (1975-79), S.L.Sharma (1979-82), M.L.Kampani (1982-85), T.S.Oberoi (1985-1990), Lt.General (Retd)R.S.Dayal (1990-92), B.N.Singh (1992), Lt.General (Retd)R.S.Dayal (1992-

93), Vakkam Purushothaman (1993-96), Dr. Rajendra Kumari Bajpai (1996), Dr. M. Channa Reddy (1996), Iswari Prasad Gupta (1996-2001), N.N.Jha (2001-04), Prof. R.G.Kapse (2004-05), Lt.General (Retd)M.M.Lakhera (2005), Prof. R.G.Kapse (2005-06), Lt.General (Retd) M.M.Lakhera (2006) to Lt.General (Retd) Bhopinder Singh (2006 to till date). Analytically we may conclude that there had been a wide variation in the policies and attitudes adopted towards welfare of the Jarawa from time to time. At one time efforts to capture them were in vogue but now the authority is seriously thinking in context of their right to freedom. The changing circumstances and increased understanding about the Jarawas through a large 'thinktank' with involvement of various departments, agencies, anthropologists, sociologists and other experts helped the recent administrators to make policies and good decisions for the island aborigines. "Let it not be said by future generations that the Indian republic has been built on the destruction of the green earth and the innocent tribals who have been living there for centuries". (President of India, 2001, Republic Day eve address).

Under the present policy the Andaman and Nicobar Administration does not allow itself to be rushed into any hasty ill- conceived program which would have an undesirable effect on the self-reliance and culture of the Jarawa, the foragers. The fact is well understood that they are not at all uninvited guests, they have equal rights like any other citizen of India for protection of life and personal liberty and the local administration has followed certain policy raising the level of nutrition and the standard living and to improve the health without disturbing the tribes adversely.

As result of the change in the administrtative attitude in the recent decades, in July'2000 through a circular from Director (Tribal Welfare), addressing the Jarawa tribe as 'hostile' has completely been banned.

For the first time a policy on the Jarawa tribe was formulated by the Central Government in the Ministry of

Home Affairs notified through Andaman and Nicobar Gazette No 210 dated December 21, 2004.

Apart from the Jarawa Policy of 2004, for protection of the forest rights, the Scheduled Tribes and Other Traditional Forest Dwellers (Recognition of Forest Rights) Act 2006, No.2 of 2007 is one of the important safeguards introduced for welfare of the forest dwellers.

The Jarawa Reserve has undergone some major amendments from time to time in exercise of the powers conferred by some of the sections and sub-sections in the Andaman and Nicobar Islands (Protection of Aboriginal Tribes) Regulation, 1956.

The Andaman and Nicobar Administration has declared various places as reserved area under the Protection of Aboriginal Tribes Regulation. Accordingly, the places designated as reserved area are the ward reserved for the Jarawas at Primary Health Centre, Tushnabad, comprising an area of 100 sq meters in survey No 103/1 at village Muslim Basti located in western side to the existing PHC building. The ward reserved for the Jarawas in the first floor of the special ward of the GB Pant Hospital connected by a staircase from the ground floor of the special ward and the ward reserved for the Jarawas at Primary Health Centre, Kadamtala comprising an area of 250 sq. meters in Survey No 1/6 at village Shantanu located on western side to the existing PHC building and connected by a concrete path have also been reserved for this purpose. Thus the Jarawa Reserve after inclusion of the medical wards has been increased from 847 to 1028 sq. kms. What is the concept of 'Reservation of Land' for the vulnerable Jarawas ? The words and concepts of Borders or Bounadaries and their Limitations formulated for them have no meaning for them if not honestly implemented. We should not try to fair our data only. The historical incidents and the available evidences suggest that from the process of colonization they smelled a threat to their extinction as result of forest clearing and population influx into their shrinking territory. Despite a number of amendments in the notification of the Jarawa Reserve, we have yet to work on it more sensitively and honestly.

Meanwhile (while writing this book) a draft of the THE ANDAMAN AND NICOBAR ISLANDS (PROTECTION OF ABORIGINAL TRIBES) AMENDMENT REGULATION, 2010 has been posted on the Adminsitrative web site (www.and.nic.in) in July 2010 and a debate has already started among the different sections of the people on buffer Zone issues.

Even before coming into the force of the Andaman & Nicobar (Protection of Aboriginal Tribes) Regulation, 1956 and the notifying of the Jarawa Reserve area in 1957 the Jarawas were well aware of the limit of their territory and in any manner never allowed intrusion of the outsiders into their vicinity. In 1950 a woman namely Sonalaxmi Chakraborty, wife of a teacher Manikanto Chakraborty, a resident of Tirur village was killed by the Jarawas while she was fishing in a nallah in the Jarawa territory. The numerous cases of similar nature in pre-1956 reflect the conflict of boundaries between the settlers and the forest dwellers.

A settler killed by the Jarawas in 1950

Pronob

The creation of Jarawa Protection Police has its genesis in Bush Police established in 1905 with an intension to keep undisturbed the habitat of the Jarawas. However with the passage of time it became in fact the Settler Protection Force. The policemen used to drive away the Jarawa with their gun shots either in air or on the natives. On 20-10-1991 the Jarawas attacked on a policeman of Bush Police and killed him in the camp at Jirkatang in south Andaman. The Jarawas always distrusted 'Khaki men' means 'staff(s) of Police or Forest'. They had a feeling of anger against the Police (Bush Police) for their unnecessary gunshots and against the Forest worker for their tree-felling. The elephants and their mahouts of the Deaprtment of Forest were also targeted. Mahauts John Xalxo, Nelson Soreng were injured while Elligus Tigga and many others were killed by the natives. For this reason the common villagers of the adjacent settlements always used to avoid wearing Khaki clothes while on move near the Jarawa Reserve. Very interesting but very important to note that the Jarawas were highly skilled to identify one. I spent a long part of my childhood at Mathura of South Andaman in the home of my grandfather Late Nibaran Chandra Bose (mother's father), situated near a Government run Primary School. Then the school uniform of the students was Khaki shirt with Khaki pant. The pupils used to come from Mathura, Alipur, Kadakachang, and Brindaban. All these villages were frequented by the Jarawa attacks. The children mostly from poor families even after schooling would play and sleep wearing the school uniforms. But the natives never targeted any student for his khaki clothing.

In the month of September 1992 about more than 250 residents gathered to protest at Port Blair against the scheme of their resettlement near the Jarawa Reserve under administrative plan to extend the airport.

In November 1993 five fishermen were killed by the Jarawas and their mutilated bodies were found in the Jarawa

Reserve at Foul Bay on western part of the Andamans. Out of a long list of known and unknown cases of poaching in the Jarawa areas a few cases only after arrests of the offenders and attacks of the Jarawas have officially been registred under ANPATR. Some of such cases are mentioned below.

Some cases registered under section 7/8 under PAT Regulation 1956 by the Andaman and Nicobar Police.

1. On 13/02/1996 at 1500 Hrs. 6 Persons R/o Phooltala, Middle Andaman apprehended by the Police while fishing at Phooltala Jungle in the Jarawa Reserve.
2. On 12/07/1996 at 0900Hrs. 3 Persons R/o Yetarjig Jungle, M/Andaman apprehended by the Police while fishing at Yetarjig No.11(Jungle Khaadi) in the Jarawa Reserve.
3. On 16/09/1996 at 0915Hrs. 5 Persons R/o Artarji, M/Andaman apprehended by the Police while fishing in Artarji Forest 8 Kms North in the Jarawa Reserve. An amount of Rs.400/- fine imposed on the offenders.
4. On 16/09/1996 at 0900Hrs. 2 Persons R/o Artarji, M/Andaman apprehended by the Police at Purlobjig No.3 Forest area, 7Kms North in the Jarawa Reserve.
5. On 14/12/1996 at 1600 Hrs. five Persons, R/o Malapuram, S/Andaman and one person from Writemyo, S/Andaman and one person R/o Mile Tilak, S/Andaman apprehended by the Police while fishing at Jirkatang No.7 at 32 Km North in the Jarawa Reserve.
6. On 12/02/1997 at 1600Hrs. 7 Persons R/o Phooltala, M/Andaman apprehended by the Police at Phooltala about 10 Kms.North in the Jarawa Reserve.
7. On 17/03/1997 at CP Nallah, Tirur No 4 in an attack by a group of Jarawas. The poachers namely Gopali

Ojha S/o Late Bhuvan Ojha R/o Herbertabad was injured while Dwijober Chowkidar R/ Templemyo was killed.

8. On 22/04/1997 at 0015Hrs. 4 Persons R/o Bamboo Tikri, M/Andaman apprehended by the Police while fishing near Spike Island 35 Km. South in the Jarawa Reserve.

9. On 21/07/1998 at 1700Hrs. 2 Persons R/o Uttara, M/ Andaman apprehended by the Police while fishing at Lakralungta 10 KM South, Middle Andaman in the Jarawa Reserve.

10. On 27/09/1998 at 1100 Hrs. 10 Persons R/o Karmatang, Mayabunder apprehended by the Police while fishing near Flat Island at 50 KM East in the Jarawa Reserve.

11. On 09/10/1998 2 Persons from Tusnabad apprehended by the Police while fishing at Flower Point, Tirur No.4 20Km North West in the Jarawa Reserve.

12. On 15/12/1998 at 1000 Hrs. 5 Persons R/o Shantipahad, M/Andaman apprehended by the Police while fishing near Bluff Island 35 Km South in the Jarawa Reserve.

13. On 08/09/1999 at 1600 Hrs. 4 Persons R/o Junglighat, Port Blair apprehended by the Police while fishing at Lakralungta, M/Andaman in the Jarawa Reserve.

14. On 08/09/1999 at 1630 Hrs. 4 Persons, R/o Junglighat, Port Blair apprehended by the Police while fishing near Spike Island, M/Andaman in the Jarawa Reserve.

15. On 20/11/1999 at 1600 Hrs. 3 Persons R/o Dhobi Basti, Mayabunder, M/Andaman apprehended by the Police

while fishing near Spike Island 12 Km South in the Jarawa Reserve.

16. On 21/11/1999 at 1100 Hrs. 3 Persons R/o Mayabunder, M/Andaman apprehended by the Police while fishing at Lakralungta, 10 Km South in the Jarawa Reserve.

17. On 21/12/1999 at 1450 Hrs. 2 Persons R/0 Kadamtala, M/Andaman apprehended by the Police at YettarJig No.10, 4Km NorthWest in the Jarawa Reserve.

18. On 22/12/1999 at 0830 Hrs. 2 Persons R/0 Kadamtala, M/Andaman apprehended by the Police at YettarJig No.10, 4Km North West in the Jarawa Reserve.

19. On 09/02/2000 at 0430 Hrs. 6 Persons R/o Mayali apprehended by the Police while fishing near Spike Island, 30 Km East in the Jarawa Reserve.

20. On 16/03/2000 2 Persons. All R/o Namunaghar,S/Andaman apprehended by the Police while fishing at Tirur No.4 16Km North West in the Jarawa Reserve

21. On 16/03/2000 at 0700 Hrs 2 Persons of Collinpur, S/Andaman apprehended by the Police while fishing at Tirur No.4 16Km North West in the Jarawa Reserve. On the same day another two persons from Namunaghar were apprehended while fishing in the Jarawa reserve.

22. On 06/04/2000 at 1430 Hrs. 2 Persons of PortMout, S/Andaman apprehended by the Police while fishing at Tirur No.4 15Km North West in the Jarawa Reserve.

23. On 06/09/2000 at 0830 Hrs. 3 Persons R/0 Kadamtala, M/Andaman apprehended by the Police while fishing in Kataidera forest, 4Km West in the Jarawa Reserve.

24. On 04/12/2000 at 0500 Hrs. 2 Persons from PortMout, S/Andaman apprehended by the Police while fishing at Tirur No.4 16Km North West in the Jarawa Reserve.

25. On 14/02/2001 at 1630 Hrs. 3 Persons R/o Panighat, Hopetown, S/Andaman apprehended by the Police while fishing near Spike Island, 30 Km East in the Jarawa Reserve.

26. On 26/02/2001 at 1500 Hrs. 3 Persons R/o Junglighat, Port Blair apprehended by the Police while fishing at Lakralungta, 15 Km West, M/Andaman in the Jarawa Reserve.

27. On 26/03/2001 at 1700 Hrs. 2 Persons of Caddlegunj, S/Andaman Apprehended by the Police while fishing at Flower Point ,Tirur No.4 16Km North West in the Jarawa Reserve.

28. On 26/03/2001at 1715 Hrs. 4 Persons of Herbertabad, S/Andaman and one person R/o Manpur apprehended by the Police while fishing at Ghasskhadi, Tirur 16Km North West in the Jarawa Reserve.

29. On 26/03/2001 at 1730 Hrs. 2 Persons from Namunaghar, S/Andaman apprehended by the Police while fishing at Flowerpoint,Tirur 16Km North West in the Jarawa Reserve.

30. On 09/08/2001 at 1400 Hrs. 3 Persons R/o Bambootikri apprehended by the Police while fishing at Lakralungta, 12 Km West, M/Andaman in the Jarawa Reserve.

31. On 09/08/2001 at 1445 Hrs. 2 Persons R/o Flat bay, Baratang apprehended by the Police while fishing near Spike Island, 30 Km.East in the Jarawa Reserve.

32. On 14/09/2001at 1600 Hrs. 3 Persons R/o, Panighat, Hopetown, S/Andaman apprehended by the Police while fishing at Lakralungta, 10 Km East in the Jarawa Reserve.

33. On 20/11/2001at 0800 Hrs. 7 Persons of Junglighat, S/Andaman apprehended by the Police while fishing at Badabalu 75Km.N/West in the Jarawa Reserve. Before the police apprehended them the Jarawas attacked on them in which one fisherman namely M. Das was shot an arrow on his chest and he was further referred to the GB Pant Hospital at Port Blair.

34. On 20/12/2001 at 1400 Hrs. 4 Persons from Port Blair apprehended by the Police while fishing at Mahua Tekri, 20 Km North in the Jarawa Reserve.

35. On 23/12/2001at 1130 Hrs. 6 Persons R/o Junglighat, Port Blair apprehended by the Police while fishing at Chotalingbang Bay 25 Km North, (West Coast) in the Jarawa Reserve.

36. On 15/04/2002 at 0700 Hrs. 1 Person of Kaushalya Nagar, M/Andaman apprehended by the Police while fishing near Purlobjig No.15 (Bamboo Nallah) M/ Andaman in the Jarawa Reserve.

37. On 19/04/2002 at 1315 Hrs. 6 Persons R/o Junglighat, Port Blair apprehended by the Police while fishing Near Enkamaye Chadda in the Jarawa Reserve.

38. On 23/04/2002 at 1830 Hrs. 4 Persons R/o Phoenix bay, Port Blair apprehended by the Police while fishing at Lakralungta 12 Km North, M/Andaman in the Jarawa Reserve.

39. On 05/05/2002 at 1800 Hrs. 5 Persons R/o Junglighat, S/Andaman apprehended by the Police while fishing at Chotabalu,35 Km N/west in the Jarawa Reserve.

40. On 05/05/2002 at 1830 Hrs. 7 Persons R/o Lohabarik, Wandoor S/Andamanapprehended by the Police while fishing at Chotabalu,35 Km N/west in the Jarawa Reserve.

41. On 23/07/2002 at 1800 Hrs. 3 Persons, 2R/oHerbertabad, 1R/o Collinpur, S/Andaman apprehended by the Police while fishing at Jhaukona Flower Point 25Km west in the Jarawa Reserve.

42. On 03/10/2002 at 0630 Hrs. one person of Namunaghar, S/Andaman apprehended by the Police while fishing at Jhaukona 25 Km west in the Jarawa Reserve.

43. On 03/10/2002 at 0640 Hrs. one Person from Collinpur, S/Andaman apprehended by the Police while fishing at Jhaukona 25 Km west in the Jarawa Reserve.

44. On 19/10/2002 at 0630 Hrs. 2 Persons R/o Collinpur, S/Andaman apprehended by the Police while fishing at Jhaukona 20 Km west in the Jarawa Reserve.

45. On 28/07/2003 two persons, R/o Kadamtala apprehended by the Police while fishing at Lakralungta 12 Km North, M/Andaman in the Jarawa Reserve.

46. On 28/7/2003 at 0815 Hrs. 2 persons R/o Kadamtala apprehended by the Police while fishing at Jhulan Pathar, Near Bamboo Tikri, Kadamtala in the Jarawa Reserve.

47. On 01/08/2003 at 1330 Hrs. one person R/o Phooltala, Kadamtala apprehended by the Police while fishing at Dhani Nallah, Kadamtala in the Jarawa Reserve.

48. On 13/8/2003 at 1500 hrs one person R/o Atarjig, Kadamtala apprehended by the Police while fishing

at Koran Nallah, Artarjig No.11, Kadamtala in the Jarawa Reserve.

49. On 2/9/2003 at 1100 hrs 2 persons R/o Artarjig, Kadamtala apprehended by the Police while fishing at Artarji Nallah, Kadamtala in the Jarawa Reserve.

50. On 29/10/2003 at 1600 hrs one person from Shantipur, Kadamtala apprehended by the Police while fishing at Jhulan Pathar, Near Bamboo Tikri, Kadamtala in the Jarawa Reserve.

51. On 3/12/2003 at 2110 Hrs. 2 person R/o Collinpur, S/Andaman apprehended by the Police while fishing in sea at Jhaukona in the Jarawa Reserve.

52. On 18/12/2003 at 1230 hrs three persons from Artarjig Kadamtala apprehended by the Police while fishing at Lakralungta, Middle Andaman in the Jarawa Reserve.

53. On 18/12/2003 at 1330 hrs 2 persons R/o Artarjig Kadamtala apprehended by the Police while fishing near Shanti pur Kadamtala in the Jarawa Reserve.

54. On 18/12/2003 at 1430 hrs 2 persons R/o Kadamtala apprehended by the Police while fishing at Bamboo Tikri, Kadamtala in the Jarawa Reserve.

55. On 6/01/2004 at 1630 Hrs. 2 person R/o Midnapur, S/Andaman apprehended by the Police while entering unauthorisely in a nallah in forest at Tirur in the Jarawa Reserve.

56. On 8/01/2004 at 0730 Hrs. 2 perosn R/o Brindaban & Ferrargunj apprehended by the Police while collecting the forest products at Hajaribagh jungle near Ferrargunj in the Jarawa Reserve.

57. On 1/04/2004 at 1030 hrs one person R/o Kadamtala apprehended by the Police while fishing at Jhulan

Pathan, near Bamboo Tikri, Kadamtala in the Jarawa Reserve.

58. On 6/04/04 at around 1030 hrs two persons R/o Kadamtala apprehended by the Police while fishing at Kulo Nallah, Artarjig, Kadamtala in the Jarawa Reserve.

59. On 14/04/2004 at 1500 Hrs. one person R/o Tirur, S/ Andaman apprehended by the Police while fishing at Tirur, Singi dabla in the Jarawa Reserve.

60. On 20/04/2004 at 1300 Hrs. 4 persons from AOOZ Naohark Co-operative Housing Society, Mumbai & one Omni driver from Shadipur apprehended by the Police while entering 1 A, Khati kona, Tirur in the Jarawa Reserve.

61. On 30/4/2004 at 1130 hrs 2 persons R/o Artarji, Kadamtala apprehended by the Police while fishing at Balu Nallah, Artarjig, Kadamtala in the Jarawa Reserve.

62. On 01/05/2004 at 1430 Hrs. 2 perons, R/o Collinpur & Manpur apprehended by the Police while fishing at Jhaukona in the Jarawa Reserve.

Some Jarawa Incidents with the Forest Workers

1. On 22/03/1989 Shri. Katrina Lakra, a forest labourer was missed from Jirkatang, South Andaman in the Jarawa area.

2. On 02/06/1991 at about 1110 Hrs. Shri.John Xalxo S/o Shri. Sukra, Mahaut went into the Jarawa Reserve near Jirkatang, South Andaman in search of a missed elephant namely Vijay Bahadur belonging to the Department of Forest in the Jarawa area. A group of Jarawas attacked on him and as a result of which his right hand and index finger were injured.

3. On 30/11/1995 at 0930 Hrs. Shri. Nelson Soreng (46), a forest worker from Putatang Extraction camp, Jirkatang, South Andaman went into the Jarawa Reserve in search of a missed elephant of the Department of Forest in the Jarawa area. A group of Jarawas attacked on him and as a result of which his left hand and waist were injured and disabled for further work.

4. On 01/03/1996 at 1100 Hrs. Shri. Advaiah (M49), Mazdoor from Putatang Regeneration Camp, South Andaman went for collection of ballies and in a Jarawa attack received injury on his left hand.

5. On 28/03/1996 at 0830 Hrs. Shri. Ladho Xess, F.P.F (52) from Punanallah Summer Extraction Area, South Andaman died of a Jarawa attack while working. The Jarawas took with them 410 Muskets with ammunition.

6. On 28/03/1996 at 0830 Hrs. Shri.Elligus Tigga S/o Shri. Ignace, Mahout (M34) from Putatang Extraction Camp, South Andaman was found dead on 29/03/1996, the next day of his missing. He was buried at Mathura, South Andaman.

7. On 28/03/1996 at 0830 Hrs. Shri.V.Jogulu (M51) from Potatang Extraction Camp, South Andaman received injury on his left wrist in a Jarawa attack.

8. On 22/12/1997 at 1230 Hrs. Shri. P.Simadri from Miletilak Forest Camp, South Andaman was found dead in the backside of Miletilak Forest Camp caused by a Jarawa attack (Signs of the Jarawa attack was found on the spot in the investigation).

In addition to the above incidents, let me mention few more cases of serial attacks during January - April 1998 which helps us study the circumstances and characteristics of the

Jarawa attacks in which both foreign and local poachers were killed.

In 1979, a Bengali contractor was given the contract of bringing sand from Long Island. Instead he began lifting sand from the Jarawa territory. The Jarawas were watching the contractor and his labourers for few days. Finally, one day they attacked the labourers and killed two of them. The contractor was badly injured and both his legs had to be amputated.

In an unusual incident of its type, during the last week of January,1998 the Jarawas attacked a group of 11 Myanmarese poachers who intruded into their territory in the west coast of Tirur village in South Andaman. Five of them were found to be dead and six were missing.

On 2nd February, 1998 the Jarawas had attacked the Tirur Outpost IV injuring a Police Constable and after two days in their second attack on 5th February, 1998 they killed an old lady of Tirur. After three days in their third attack on 09 February, 1998 they killed one Shri. Jogin Chakraborty of Ferrargunj.

On 23/04/1998, a Jarawa attack was made in Jirkatang area when one Shri. Balakrishnan, R/o Jirkatang No 2 reportedly went into the Jarawa Reserve forest to collect Ballies for making fence on his land. He was shot down by the Jarawas and he died on the spot. The case was registered under section 302/34/IPC at PS Bambooflat. After this Jarawa incident no such case has been recorded for a long time to go. In the meantime the Jarawas were voluntarily coming out to contact the outsiders in peacefull manner. This case I took as a very special case in the behavioural study of the Jarawas. In the year 2004 I was deputed at Jirkatang area of South Andaman to conduct systematic study on the Jarawas and execute the other Jarawa welfare activities as employee of the Andaman Adim Janjati Vikas Samiti, Port

Blair. I was allotted a quarter in premises of a primary school at Jirkatang2 and fortunately the widow of Late Balakrishnan and her three sons were my neighbours. After coming into a familiar relationship with them they freely told me what actually had happened on that day when Shri Balakrishnan was killed by the Jarawas. The sons of Late Balakrishnan namely Ajay, Vijay and Sanjay had no expression of anger against the Jarawas when they told me how their father was killed by the native forest dwellers. Shri Balakrishnan working as Mazdoor in the Forest department was a daring hunter. He was staying near the Jarawa Reserve at Jirkatanag No 2. Quite often he used to pitch hunting trap to hunt the deer/wild boar in the Jarawa Reserve near a nallah. One day a wild boar was trapped in his hunting trap. When his teenaged two sons namely Ajay and Vijay went to see the wild boar and tried to remove it from the trap, few armed Jarawas who were positioned behind a bush started throwing of stones and wood pieces towards the boys but did not shoot arrows to kill them. The boys rushed to their house and reported about the incidence to their father. The clever father waited for hours and then lost his patience and moved to get the prey from his trap followed by his sons. When he reached the spot he received a shower of arrows from the Jarawas. At this time too they (Jarawas) did not harm the boys. The hunter Balakrishnan ran to escape himself but finally he fell down near a tree. The boys further explained how their father was killed and his body was brutally mutilated by the Jarawas. The natives removed the eye balls of the dead hunter.

During the period when I was collecting data from various Police Outposts and Police Stations I was surprised enough that many cases of killing and injuries of settlers which I knew from the settlers and the Jarawas were not lodged by the family members of the victims with the police. Perhaps they had a fear to be executed under the ANPAT regulations because all those cases occurred within the notified Jarawa Reserve.

After the killing of Balakrishnan there has been a long chronological gap of silence in context of the Jarawa killings. However many incidents of Jarawa killings were reported by the poachers and the Jarawas themselves but lacked solid evidences. Recently in the year 2008 a case of murder in Jarawa Reserve was registered in which a Jarawa named Hoteile was killed at Mahua Tekri near Kadamtala by a group of fishers (and hunters?). On the day of the grave incident few fishermen intruded into the Jarawa territory on west coast and camped at one place near a Jarawa camp. A group of Jarawa came and asked for food when they were cooking. In the meantime as the Jarawas reported that the fishermen threw boiled water on one of the Jarawas. A fight was ensued between them in which Hoteile and a fisherman were killed.

My enquiry from the villagers and from the Jarawas corroborated the fact that all the Jarawa incidents happened just as acts of protection of their resources and/or revenge and/or self defence. The poachers often entered the reserve mainly to hunt spotted deer and wild boar, to fish, to collect forest produces such as wood, bamboo, honey. resin and pan leaves. On many occasions they destroyed Jarawa huts, molestated Jarawa women and snatched their belongings such as pig, baskets, resin, honey and whatever they find of their use in absence of adult male members. Reactively the annoyed and angry Jarawas entered the adjacent non-Jarawa settlements mainly at moonlit night in search of their target poacher and in course of the search they took with them their needs from the settlements like banana ('chone'), vessel ('busu'), tools and implements and iron pieces ('taah') etc. and killed the animals to satisfy themselves. It is worthy to mention that on many occasions the poachers had destroyed the Jarawa huts by burning them but the Jarawas never in revenge tried to burn the houses of villagers, while during that period almost all the houses were built of wood, bamboo and other forest materials. Secondly the Jarawas when on move in forests used to beat tree buttresses (local villagers called 'Pankha maar') to produce sound cautioning the non-Jarawas if present near to them. The Jarawas in whole of their history never killed anybody unreasonably. Most importantly the Jarawas since the first penal settlement have never permitted anyone to cut tree in their forests. The Jarawas further disclosed that on some cases they (poachers) cruelly beheaded their children when mothers put their babies in sand holes upto shoulder or neck to keep control over their movement and went to fish at a distance. Many old poachers with help of their 12 bore guns licensed by the administration for protection against a Jarawa attack ably killed the Jarawas in their poaching activities. These are few main reasons of the reasons for which whenever a poacher was killed his/her body was found brutally mutilated in anger by the Jarawas. The neighbouring tribes Great Andamanese also used to mutilate the bodies in anger. On 4th March 1858 they killed two Britishers when they tried to have fun with their women and on 28th June 1863 killed Mr. Pratt, a Naval Brigadesman who tried to rape a tribal woman. In both the cases the dead bodies were mutilated beyond recovery. In some cases of Jarawa killings the bodies were found cut into several pieces including the genitals with intestines and eyeballs pulled out. When they had to kill a poacher near to their habitat they immediately drag out the body after killing and place the corpse near outskirt of village. It was also indicated on some occasions that they mutilated the bodies according to their own customs. For example 1) They damaged jaw of the dead and 2) they detached the limbs of the dead and placed the same on a high ground. The Onges of Little Andaman performed their death rituals after killings in the same way. After I took charges of the Onge settlement and began to work on them in July 2006, I discovered that the

Onges do perform the same ritual as the Jarawas do. Further I discovered that the Onges and the Jarawas have close cultural and linguistic affinities.

The local poachers constantly compelled them to continue their trend of hostility and attacks as self-protective measure. For the said reasons the Jarawa attacks continued even after the Jarawas understood well that all the outsiders are not bad. They never misbehaved with AAJVS staffs and always kept trust on them. They send their women and children with the AAJVS staffs for medical treatment.

3

The Enmen Story

The situation took a dramatic turn in the history of Jarawa contact when a Jarawa boy aged 14 years namely Enmen alias Teriyaatahaawuwe (not Enmei alias Diryatohuwa as spelled by one anthropologist) was found with his leg fractured in a nallah near the house of Shri Bijay Baroi S/o Late Paresh Baroi at Attenjig Corner in Kadamtala on 15th April 1996. The incident of the Jarawa boy sustaining multiple fractures was not a fall-out of any scuffle with the local population but it was simply an accident. In the early morning when Shri Bijay Baroi saw the Jarawa boy screaming in pain in the nallah he rushed to him. He carried the boy to his house, gave drinking water and some first aid treatment and carried him to the Primary Health Centre at Kadamtala. During the period of his treatment at Port Blair the official side served the best services with additional care to Enmen in respect of food and behaviour.

Meanwhile, for the first time in the history of the Jarawa contact four Jarawa boys were befriended near Bluff Bay in South Andaman. This occurred when the members of the contact team of the Administration on their way back after contacting the Jarawas at LakeraLungta in Middle Andaman tried to contact the Jarawas in South Andaman and found these four Jarawa boys waving at them from the shore near Bluff Bay. Two of the Jarawa boys swam towards the boat of the contact team and gleefully accepted the gifts. Hitherto a small group of Jarawa (of only Middle Andaman) were being contacted and this was for the first time that the Jarawa of South Andaman could be brought into contact.

Over here at Port Blair the hospitalized Jarawa boy Enmen was convalescing in the G.B.Pant Hospital. He received large number of gift items from officers, nurses, staffs of the hospital and other visitors. Someone gave him a mirror which he used to hold at different angles to see his image therein. He sometimes used to look behind the mirror to meet the other Enmen. When a group photograph of the previous contact was shown to him, he started crying perhaps in memory of his people. Films of Donald duck, Micky Mouse, Tarzen were shown to him for his amusement. From all sides several eyes were fixed at his window to catch a glimpse of the boy. After his successful treatment for about six months in the hospital he was released with plenty of gift items among his group at Foul Bay at the western coast of Andamans on October 4, 1996. A sullen expression mingled with joy of being re-united with his family members were emanating from the face of Enmen when he returned to his retreat in the thickets of Middle Andaman after about six months with plenty of presents given by the Andaman & Nicobar Administration. Enmen was received by his parents alongwith 65 other Jarawas soon after the official party landed at Foul Bay. Contrary to the obscure belief, the young Jarawa received a warm welcome on his arrival by his fellow beings and his parents were seen moved to happy tears at the home coming of their son. The father took him in his lap and sat quietly for hours in their traditional way of welcoming. After about a year the Jarawas started coming out of their forest in groups. This phenomenon has minimized the administrative expedition to befriend the Jarawa. During this period nobody predicted what was stored in the pocket of future.

For the first instance of its sort in the history of Andamans, the Jarawa came out of their native forest in the open amidst the so-called civilized population. This incident happened on October 21, 1997 when 8 Jarawas (four of them were females) came out of their habitat of Lakera Lungta. Again on October 22, two Jarawas came out. In such cases they were provided with the gift items on administration behalf. Again in the morning of Octobar 24, the residents of the area were taken by surprise when they saw as many as 31 Jarawas appeared at the Uttara Jetty. The police personnel after providing food in adequate quantity to them dropped them back to the forest of Lakeralungta. A police boat, M.V.Sahayak left for Uttara jetty from Port Blair with food articles provided by the Directorate of Tribal Welfare for the Jarawas. These were the first instances in the whole history of the isles when the Jarawa voluntarily sought to establish contact with the settlers and ventured out of the forest and into the mainstream settlements. Some experts explain that Enmen developed a cultural affinity to the outside world; in their view Enmen perhaps wanted others of his community to experience the outsiders' hospitality that he had received. It is this, which brought the Jarawa out of the forest. To them this was "Enmen Revolution". The media and others have also written much on the Enmen episode rhetorically. For sometimes when I was at the infancy stage of my research on them the same impression was in my mind. But, as result of my continuous research on them and my association with the authority, I now understand deeply the facts and the circumstances of that time which compelled the Jarawas to come out. But nobody knows better than the Jarwas, I firmely believe. It may also be mentioned that the Jarawa boy Enmen and his wife had been introduced to the then Hon'ble Prime Minister Shri. Atal Behari Vajpayee at

Port Blair on 1st January 1999. In recent years I have observed that Enmen very rarely came out of the forest abode to contact the people. He came only occasionally seeking medical treatment or as attendant of sick group member. In my long years of research work I never saw him leading his group in contacting the outsiders. It is noteworthy that nobody from the Jarawa community told me that Enmen brought them out. Before Enmen many Jarawas had experienced good hospitality of the outside world but they did not lead their fellow members to come out of forest and contact the people. There is one more case recorded in the history similar to the case of Enmen. A Jarawa man namely Talai was found injured in a fight on 25th March 1884. He received good hospitality like Enmen and after his recovery he was taken by Mr. Portman in a contact expedition but the Jarawas never came in friendly contact. The Jarawa man Talai absconded himself when Mr. Portman was yet to come close to his fellows. In the year 1968 few Jarawas were brought to Port Blair. A good course of hospitality they experienced in few days at Port Blair. After reaching back to their habitat they found no place for them in their own community. The Jarawa did not repeat 'the 1884 and 1968' in case of Enmen but treated him in other way of Negligence. The Enmen had no role in the Jarawa's coming out. From the chronological study of the incidents it is evident that the concept of so-called Enmen Revolution is purely baseless and false. Enmen was released at his forest home after his treatment in GB Pant Hospital on 04-10-1996. The Jarawa group for the first time came out of forests to contact people voluntarily on 21-10-1997. Does it mean that the Enmen had to take more than one year to convince his people to come out? If yes then why Enmen did not lead his group from the front in the first contact of their history? Why Enmen has reserved himself in the hinterland? Why Shri Balakrishnan was killed on 23-04-1998 by the Jarawas even after their first such friendly contact? It is apparent that there was no link between the

Enmen episode and the First friendly contact by the Jarawas themselves as gossiped and documented.

- Enmen found injured : 15 April 1996
- Enmen admitted in hospital : 16 April 1996
- Enmen after discharged from hospital and released at home : 04 October 1996
- A Jarawa group for the first time in history came out of the forests to contact the people : 21 October 1997
- In the old series of human killing by the Jarawa the last killing of an outsider at Jirkatang on : 23 April 1998

On the subject once I wanted to get reaction from Enmen himself who was then camped at PHC Kadamtala. He remained mute while the other Jarawas briefed that during that period large number of Myanmarese and Thai poachers were active with their guns in the forests. There were a number of skirmishes and battles between the natives and the poachers. But whether such situation compelled them to come out of their abode forests in broad day light not confirmed. It was also reported by the people that they came out of forests in hunger and there was food starvation in their forests. That's why they gleefully accepted the bananas gifted by the villagers. Such people are still advocating for giving Jarawas plenty of bananas. I am surprised how the Jarawas are reported to be banana dependants? Are the tribes who were living in the forests for thousands of years were and are living on bananas in the forests? Can anyone show me a naturally grown single banana plant in the Jarawa Reserve? If there is a dearth of food in forest, then they should have died long back. In their territory they find abundantly the animal based diet items like wild boar, crab, fishes, water monitor, prawns, mussels, crustaceans, bivalve molluscs, shells, turtle eggs, honey and larvae of honey bee etc. further supplemented by varieties of plant based food which are rich in carbohydrates and vitamins. Many wild fruits (Keen, Jiggi, Epogotang, uejao, Bagatho, Dou, gee, Tehat, etc), roots and tubers are also included in their dietary menu. In case of food starvation in their forests before coming out of forests in hunger they could have consumed many items which they never consumed so far such as eel fishes, birds, Andaman teal, deer and many other things that can be consumed by us or by them in a madness of hunger. The recent studies have also revealed that there is no shortage of food for the Jarawas in their reserve. However, years before attempts have been made for sea ranching, banana plantation and other horticultural plantation in the Jarawa Reserve for augmenting food resources for the Jarawas. Such things which may harm the ecological equilibrium of the tropical rain forests should not be introduced in future.

As a sprouting result of the first friendly contacts, largely their movements on Andaman Trunk Road (ATR) and towards the adjacent settlements have been increased. Some accepted rides on the vehicles going through the Andaman Trunk Road. Fewer Jarawa began to construct their huts on the roadside. There are few major huts constructed by the Jarawa on ATR side such as 'Tullichada', 'Bimuchada', and 'Tuichada' of South Andaman and 'Levchada' at Dhaninallah of Middle Andaman. When Jarawas of one habitat killed any big prey then the Jarawas of other habitat(s) come to get share in the feast. This is another important reason for their movement from one habitat to another. Now they began to board tops of buses and trucks to reach the destination (Jarawa habitat) to eat pork ('Wowe') or to reach any forest/sea location to hunt/fish or for other purposes. The Andaman Administration has made all efforts at possible level to stop the Jarawas from boarding the vehicles. They started begging for whatever they see of their interest from the people on ATR and other contact points. This trend never reduced.

As result of the modern modes of treatment and hospitality with providing of amenities, the Jarawa members began to use soap, hair oil and towels, while many of them started wearing clothes and bathing properly. The hospital and PHCs have become a good ground for our observation of such practices of the Jarawa.

It was an important date noted in my personal daily diary when on 17 July 2000 I got appointment in the AAJVS and it was the first time when on 05/08/2000 I was deputed to take 09 Jarawas from GB Pant Hospital, Port Blair and release them at their habitat at RK Nallah, South Andaman. These 09 Jarawas who were discharged from the hospital were for all time staring at this new face. I was fascinated by the sight of the Jarawas in their natural surroundings for the first time in my life having a jungle trek in their reserve. Nothing can match the excitement of sighting something you have been anticipating for years. Looking to their strange aggressiveness my blood was frozen throughout the journey. I never saw them in such aggressiveness in my next direct contacts with them. Now I understand what is a difference between a strange man and a friend for the Jarawas. The similar behaviour I received from the Jarawas of Middle Andaman when contacted for the first time on 12/08/2000 when I escorted in the way 05 Jarawas discharged from the G B Pant Hospital, Port Blair and released them at PHC Kadamtala. The behavioural aspect of the Jarawas has been one of the most interesting aspects I feel from my experiences vary from one situation to another. But normally you find them amiable. It was 18 Nov 2000 when for the first time I understood that controlling the Jarawa movement to prevent their intrusion into the adjacent settlements without having friendly relationship with them is really a Herculean task. It was reported to the office of the Executive Secretary, AAJVS, Port Blair that few young Jarawas made intrusion into the villages of Tirur and Manpur and Ranchi basti. Self with my two assisting staffs Sarfuddin and Zubair rushed to the spot and found there 6-7 young Jarawas roaming on the road with aggressive behaviour shown to the people around. As soon as they saw us they became little cold. The packets of biscuits alongwith the iron implements taken from the shops and houses were exposed from their bundles of booties. When self reached to one Jarawa youth namely Homounda and tried to persuade to return all those items taken from the villgers, he quickly replied- They come to our land and kill our pigs..I won't give these items..The boys remained adamant in the decision not to leave the road. Then self with my staffs played a humble trick with them. We came close to one of them and said – after the villagers lodged complaint we forthwith left Port Blair without having the day meal. Now we are hungry... You give us something to eat in your chadda (home). The boy calmnly listened to this and started managing his bundle to finally start walking towards a hillock where his chadda namely Lapaitala was located. We as good disciples just followed them and soon reached their hut in the dense forest in the hillock. They offered us packets of biscuit and bananas from the booty. Here it was a crystal clear for our understanding later strengthened by study of Jarawa incidences that they do not have any strong concept of ownership of food. 'Its yours and its mine' has no meaning for them. Gradually my efforts to establish friendly relationship with them were becoming successful. It further developed my confidence when I successfully tackled the Jarawas in a massive raid in broad daylight occurred on 24-11-2000 in the villages Mathura, Tusonabad and Manpur. On this day about 80 Jarawas came to the Mathura village of South Andaman in full turmoil. They looted the belongings of the villagers like vessel, iron implements, cloth and miscellaneous items. After receiving the information in the office of AAJVS, we immediately reached the spot. One group of the Jarawa disappeared in the forest near Alipur village. The 46 Jarawas were brought to the Jarawa habitat of Tirur by a Police Van. On the way when the van got little slow near a pot hole three of the Jarawas jumped down from the van and entered the settlements of Tusonabad. Myself with three Policemen with all efforts stopped them from taking plenty of goods from the houses. However the Jarawas brought with them some sickles, daos, and piece of red cloth. These three Jarawas were also brought to their habitats within hours. No outsider was injured in this case. On the next day the Jarawas were shifted by a Police truck from Tirur to the Jarawa habitat of RK Nallah area (South Andaman). As they proved earlier on many occasions, in this case too they proved how sensitive people they are. In course of their looting of items from houses many of the women folk fell down loosing their conscious in fear but the Jarawas never touched them while one of them (Jarawa) started pulling down a sickle from a bundle of straw hanging from the roof. At the moment I tried to stop him from doing so by holding his hands from back. When he pulled his hands successfully out with the sickle and in that force I got a little injury on my wrist but since it was on my vein the bleeding started rapidly. Looking to this the Jarawa before I understand anything kept aside the sickle and rushed to a bush and after a while I saw a tiny stem with few leaves in his hand. He started making paste of the leaves in his palm and forthwith applied on my injury. It wondered me that in the process of his so dedicated medical practice he had forgotten the purpose for which he entered in that house. From this date onwards my job continued to carefully control the movement of the Jarawas to prevent any untoward incidents with the settlers and passengers on the Andaman Trunk Road. On 25/05/2001 on behalf of the administration I disbursed the relief amount (70% of the loss reported) for the victim people of Manpur, Tirur, Tusonabad, Herbertabad and Collinpur against their loss of property caused by the Jarawas in the above said incident occurred on 24-11-2000 to the incumbent Pradhan Smti.Savitri Devi. It is noteworthy that the Britishers used to pay around $300-350 as compensation amount if anybody killed by the Jarawas.

Most of the times I spent in patrolling duty in the Jarawa areas and sometimes joined by one Medical Officer appointed by the AAJVS who needed an interpreter. Despite our caring and high attention, on many occasions the Jarawas proved themselves to be unpredictable. On 20-06-2001 a Jarawa patient who was admitted into the Special Ward of the GB Pant Hospital somehow absconded himself from the ward. On receipt of information I was officially sent in the search operation. I forthwith went in search of them to all parts of the city by my bike but could not find him. Finally I didn't know what prompted me to enter the Bus Terminus of Aberdeen Bazaar. To my surprise one man told me that he saw a junglee (refered to as Jarawa) on board an express bus headed towards the Kadamtala perhaps somebody helped him without which it was impossible. After about six hours it was confirmed from the Kadamtala through official source that the Jarawa safely reached the Primary Health Centre to join his fellow members admitted there. The official field functionaries stationed at Kadamtala enquired from him about how he absconded from the hospital. His explanation interpreted as - "I just told the person on duty to wait for my coming back after attending nature's call and crossed the wall of the hospital premises hiding all eyes and came to bazaar area where one person brought me near a Bus, he explained."

In July 2001 (vide office order no 178 dated 02-07-2001) I was transferred to the Strait Island to take over the charges of the Great Andamanese settlement. This was an opportunity to work as an official for the first time on the Great Andamanese who were once the largest primitive tribe in the Andaman Islands divided territorially in different bands from south to north of Andamans. In the Great Andamanese settlement on Strait Island I worked for welfare of the Great Andamanese till 26-09-2001, when again transferred from Strait Island to Port Blair to assist the officers and work on the Jarawas. On 1st March 2002 about 150 Jarawas in different groups entered the settlements of Ferrargunj, Manpur, Tirur and other settlements adjacent to the Jarawa Reserve. The Jarawas raided the house of one Shri. Rajendra Pillai R/o Manpur, South Andaman and looted the worthy belongings including the gold jewels as the victim reported. Myself immediately rushed to the field and somehow controlled the aggressive Jarawas and successfully shifted them to their habitat at Tirur. After the incident my headquarter shifted to Tirur to stop their raids and implement the welfare schemes vide office Order No. 02 dated 01-04-2002 and since then no untoward Jarawa incident could be occurred. For the period ahead I continued to render my services towards welfare of the Jarawas sometimes having headquarter at Tirur and sometimes at Jirkatang2. The official orders of shifting of headquarter did not specify to work only at that particular area but sometimes covered Tirur to Baratang including the Middle Strait. Importantly from 04/05/02 to 15/05/02 my headquarter was fixed at Tirur but I had to cover the Jarawa areas of the Tirur, the Middle Strait and the Baratang and on other hand the Strait Island towards welfare of the Great Andamanese. Such was the situation with an AAJVS worker, but this indicated the lack of working staffs.

It was my tiring but interesting task to control the outside movement of the Jarawas in the initial period of their contact. The incidents of appearance of the CURIOUS JARAWAS on the different contact points including the ATR increased with their journey of becoming 'Little Contacted Tribe' to 'Befriended Tribe'. They were so curious to know about the machinery world and for want of change in the taste of food that quite often they appeared onto the Andaman Trunk Road and the adjacent settlements to contact the people. Myself was especially deputed to keep control over their such rough mingling with the people to prevent the Jarawa exploitation and any untoward incident. The authority (Andaman Adim Janjati Vikas Samiti, Port Blair undertaken by the Andaman and Nicobar Administration) became more cautious and implemented welfare schemes very cautiously with no hasty judgment. The AAJVS staffs through their skills and the gained Jarawa vocabulary won the trust of the Jarawas and developed a harmonious relationship with them which eased their work with the natives. Their women call us as 'Mappe' (elder brother) and in civilized response we call them 'Waami' means sister. They started constructing their chaddas near the ATR which helped them as and when wished to contact the people, board the vehicles and collect the snack items thrown on road by the goers. As one of the several examples, in October, 2000 a group of Jarawas consisted of about 30 members came from Tirur and constructed a community hut right on ATR side near Punnanallah. This new habitat was called "Tulichadda" by the Jarawas. In order to attract the window passengers of buses and small vehicles they sometimes sing the Hindi songs learnt partially and the children somersault on the road. On staying of road side they have access to both sets of resources those available from the forests and those available from the road. For that reason the women joined by the children are often seen in collection of roots and tubers mostly on the road side. In course of their collection of articles thrown out from the windows of buses and other vehicles all men, women and children individually spread hands before the passengers which generate public rumor and the energy to tell us, 'the Jarawas are hungry that's why they beg before us, why don't you give them food?' By this time they became habitual to use the vehicles to reach one place to another avoiding their traditional forest path of movement. It was also observed that when in a hut a pig is brought then the Jarawas of other area come to the hut to get their share by travelling on vehicles. In 'contact with the people' comparatively the young members of the Jarawa community are much enthusiasts. Their singing, dancing and somersaulting on road became a usual scenario on the Andaman Trunk Road. At this juncture, the high attention shiftd to the Jarawas' movement on the Andaman Trunk Road while on the other hand many unnoticed and unguarded regions of the Jarawa movement were extensively used by the poachers without fear of the Jarawa attack.

4

The Regions of Dispute

At present many villages or the areas where there is no tribe but they still bear the names given by the Andamanese tribes and once came within the vicinity of their activities. Adazig of Baratang, Miletilak and Jirkatang of south Andaman etc are few examples in this context. Now these areas are lying adjacent to the Jarawa Reserve. The Bush Police staffs and local settlers named many places and demarcated the Jarawa areas with their own imaginay lines through these names. They have their own forest paths to enter the Jarawa territory and visiting officials were shown these fake boundaries and the Jarawa areas as observed in Tirur area where some settlers keep their peak efforts to save their banana, coconut and arecanut plantations grown on the encroached Jarawa areas. On many occasions I had to face their agitations when the Jarawas entered such encroached areas for the bananas. These areas are still the areas of dispute. It was also known from the Jarawas themselves that the paths on which now the outsiders often walk previously used by the Jarawas frequently. In order to re-capture their traditional paths the Jarawas used to pitch poisonous tail bones of the ray fishes and sometimes ordinary fish bones on those paths. Now the present Jarawas are not following such practices. Now some settlers are doing such things more dangerously. They started erecting fances with electric wires to protect their plantations. Interestingly in one case in 1998, a settler died of electrocution when he accidently stepped on his own electrical trap.

The main settlement areas where Jarawa incidents occurred were Herbertabad, Templemyo, Tirur, Collinpur, Manpur, Muslim Basti, Hobdaypur, CaddleGunj, Aniket, Tusonabad, Sonapahad, Caddlegunj, Ferrargunj, Jirkatang, Alipur, Mathura, Beachdera, Miletilak, Adajig, Lorojig, Oralkacha, Udaygarh, and settlements near Wraftess Creek in Baratang Island, Phooltala, Dhaninallah, Hanspuri, Chainpur, Kaushalya Nagar, Kalsi, and Shantanu in the Middle Andamans. The people of these regions in general are acrimonious, critical, and exasperated about the Jarawas and the administration in the context of Jarawa raids. Whenever any incident is occurred caused by the Jarawas the people forthwith pounce back on the local authority.

These regions of dispute were protected by the Bush Police Outposts, colonized by different ethnic groups at different times. Burmese, Moplahs and mostly the Bengali refugee settlers from the east Pakistan resettled at Tirur, Temple Myo, Herbertabad, Collinpur, and Manpur area. Tirur called 'Boiab' by the Jarawa has been one of the major parts of the island frequented by the Jarawas led to many incidents. The Tirur village situated as the last village on the western flank is compressed between Cholunga Hills and Mount Chatterton in a narrow valley about 40 Kms west of Port Blair. On the west, off Mount Chatterton is the massive westcoast hills, a reserve forest that is the primary abode of the Jarawas. The Tirur village hotspot of the Jarawas for their attacks in south Andaman settled in 1949. The villagers of Tirur had to contend with the Jarawa menace throughout the history of the village. The Tirur village is protected by police outposts interrupting the natural movement of the Jarawas. The Police outpost No 4 located at Constance Bay, Outpost 3 located between Mt Chatterton and Cholunga range and between these two outposts are outposts 1 A and Anjalinallah. Later on a number of the outposts abolished. The people of Tirur and nearby regions still recall those days when they would switch off all the lights and go to bed soon around 1900 1930 Hrs in mortal fear of the Jarawas. The common villagers lived in terror and the poachers of the same village continued to enter the Jarawa territory without fear. The villagers still recollect the incidents of Jarawa sighting, their raids and killing of people and animals. The staffs posted at the said four police outposts and altogether the villagers both directly and indirectly interrupted the free movement of the natives. Close to Tirur the Jarawas have attacked on the villagers of Collinpur, a coastal village. Few old villagers said that the tribals rarely entered the villages. There used to be encounters in the forests. The common villagers were not targeted intentionally. After their coming into our friendly contact, on several occasions they appeared in broad day light in the villages Herbertabad, Manpur, and Templemyo which are located at distance of not more then 6 kms from Tirur.

Officially, in performance of my duties gradually my main tasks began to spin around controlling such movement of the natives which may lead to rough mingiling with the people or any unpleasant incident. My mind always questioned to me after going through their kindness, honesty and hospitality that how these people could kill a person? In curiosity I then started enquiring from them about the historical incidents of their attacks on the settlements, taking their belongings and many other incidents that I during my doctoral research noted down from newspapers, books, official records and the cases known from the villagers. Since the Jarawas don't understand the date or year of event but on indication of the seasons, spots, field/ house showing, giving identical detail of victims and in acquisition of their language we enquired from the Jarawas themselves. Further, we got no difficulty to unfold the facts obscurely but to the extent it was enough to understand that behind each such incident there was a trend to protect their resources and revenge against the poachers. In course of my interrogation I was excited and hardly believing that I was amidst those ancient people who once upon a time were the subject people of my highest degree of curiosity to know about them having with me only some incidents, myths, rumours and conception created by the people about them. I began with questioning on killing of mother of one of our staffs Shri Navdeep Mondal of Tirur village. Her dead body was found badly mutilated by the Jarawas perhaps a sheer expression of their anger. The Jarawa old members replied that the lady was fishing in a nallah in their territory and they were watching her distantly for a long time. On many occasions the Jarawas threw stones on her as warning but she continued to come and fish in the nallah. Interestingly her son Shri Navdeep Mondal was also present and became mute when I sought his reaction on the Jarawa explanation.

The Bush Police camps (now Jarawa Protection Police) were assigned the tasks to protect the villagers from the Jarawa attacks. It has been reported on many occasions that they fired rounds of blank catridges into the air to scare the Jarawas when they came close to them. I personally have little doubt on it. In contrary to such statements the present Jarawas have mentioned several Jarawa deaths caused by the so called blind rounds of the Bush Police in count more than the number of actual Jarawa deaths they (BP) reported. Many of the retired APWD and Forest workers and old villagers had also confirmed this. The adjacent villages Templemyo and Collinpur were old convict settlements where Burmese convicts were settled under penal settlement during the British Regime. Apart from the Tirur the nearby villages Herbertabad, Templemyo, Collinpur and Manpur have been under serious threat of Jarawa attack at different times. There were several cases of the Jarawa raid/attack occurred in these villages; examples are –

*The Jarawas made raid in the premises of Jagdish Baroi R/o Tirur No 2 and killed a buffalo in the night of 12-07-1992,

*the incident of 12-10-1992 at Herbertabad,

*on 23-12-1994 a Jarawa raid in the garden of Ashok Biswas S/o Mahananda Biswas, R/o Herbertabad,

*on 18-05-1995 the Jarawas killed Bhaskar Sanga S/o Matis Sanga at Tirur No2,

*the Jarawas made raids in Collinpur on 13-09-1995 and 08-10-1995,

*again on 01-11-1995 the Jarawas killed Manoranjan Sarkar R/o Tirur at Tirur No 03 Nallah,

*on 03-01-1996 the Jarawas entered Tirur No 02,

*on 22-04-1997 Nukul Roy R/o Herbertabad was attacked by about 12-15 Jarawas,

*on 02-02-1998 the Jarawas attacked JPP Tirur No 04 in which Nicholas Surain PC No 1629 was injured, and

*on 05-02-1998 the Jarawas killed a lady Punmala Mondal W./o Late Narayan Mondal,etc.

The people of these villages usually engage themselves in fishing, hunting deer and wild boar and collection of wood and bamboo, the most versatile grasses grown in the Jarawa Reserve. One Jarawa hut called 'Lapaitala' is situated at only 93 Meters (On 05-04-2002 the ALHW team got measurement with their equipments) distance from the nearest point of the road at Tirur No3 passing through the JPP outpost. During my stint at Tirur village in 2002, we regularly made visits to Jhaukona marsh via Jarawa Protection Post No 04. It is very difficult to reach from the outpost to Jhaukona by a small police boat during low tide. In low tide the area becomes a perfect ground for a large number of the endemic Andaman Teal (Anas gibberifrons) to gather to rest their wings. The local people lay down hunting traps and fishing cast nets on the swamp to hunt these endangered ducks. From Manpur village ahead there is a wide range of villages from Tusonabad to Ograbraj dominated by the Moplah people in and around the Mount Tuson. The deportion and resettlement of Moplahs in Andamans began in February 1922 and ended in 1926. The other villages which are located within vicinity of the Jarawa activities are Aniket and Caddlegunj thickly populated by the Bhantus. The Bhantus of Andamans were brought and resettled from Uttar Pradesh in early 19th century by the then British Government. In UttarPradesh Bhantus were notified as a Criminal Tribe. Due to their criminal habit of theft, loot and robbery, the then British Government declared the Bhantus and other neighbouring communities such as the Baurias, the Sansias, the Haburas, the Doms, the Kanjars, the Pasis, the Salias, the Karwals, and the Nats as the Criminal Tribes under the Criminal Tribes Act (III) of 1911 (Wahi 1949 : 84). During 1926 in Andamans, some Bhantus were brought to Kalapani (Andamans) from different Indian jails. Later on, a few others who were not actually convicted voluntarily came to Andamans from the traditional Bhantu settlements. The reason behind their coming was that their relatives who were brought as convicts had been assured to roam about freely in the Andamans and were offered to build up new settlements. They were allowed to bring their wives and children also. Initially the Bhantus were kept in the Cellular Jail for few months but due to the lack of space they were shifted to Bambooflat Barracks for another few months. Under an introduced system of the British Administration those prisoners who had a good record of conduct in the jail could settle down permanently in the island as free settlers. Such prisoners were called Free Ticket Holders. They were given both agriculture and homestead land and an amount of cash advance to meet the expenditure of agriculture and maintaining family. Thus the Bhantus have been permanently settled in Andamans. The Bhantus again desired before the British authority to allow them to bring their relatives to live with them who were still in the mainland India. Those relatives were landless and in poor economic conditions. In view of these the British authority made necessary arrangement to bring those Bhantus who were in the mainland interested to settle down in these islands. Thus a large number of Bhantus came to the Andamans in 1928 comparatively more than in 1926. Bonington has stated that in the Bhantus colony of Andamans there were 285 individuals (1932: 41). Initially the Bhantus were asked to settle down in the Mathura village of Ferrargunj, Tehsil in South Andaman by the British Government. Subsequently due to some problems they were shifted to Ferrargunj and Aniket village in Ferrargunj Tehsil in South Andaman. Since they are resettled near the Jarawa territory they got a good hunting ground (Jarawa territory) for their hunting and fishing activities. In 1942 these islands were occupied by the Japanese. During the Japanese reign the life of the people was intolerable. Flogging and torturing became the order of the day under the Japanese administration. The Japanese did not allow the peoples to leave the island. But when they left the island and the British re-occupied the island in 1945 many Bhantus left these islands for fear of further torture and returned to mainland. But in the mainland when they did not find any suitable way to earn bread came back to Andamans. After coming back to Andamans they found that their old settlements had been occupied by the people of other ethnic groups. They appealed to the then government to return their previous occupancy rights over their lost settlements. The British Government then rehabilitated the Bhantus in Caddlegunj and Aniket villages. Inspite of the assistance provided by the government to earn livelihood through employment, agriculture and other schemes they continued to engage themselves in hunting activities in the Jarawa area. The Govt also gave them he-buffaloes and she- buffaloes on loan. This type of loan was locally known as 'Takabi Loan'. The Bhantu hunters used to destroy the Jarawa huts in course of their poaching activities. At the other end, many householders were issued licensed guns to protect themselves from the Jarawa attacks. This made the villagers happy that whether the Jarawa come or not no matter but they can hunt wild boar and spotted deers with help of those guns in the forests. Evidently in those villages in those days hunting expeditions were organized in the Jarawa Reserve and large quantity of venison arranged as feast in the marriage ceremonies. The poachers have well learnt the making of 12 bore bullets with help of the empty case of used bullet and the locally available materials. There on a hillock called Sonapahad an old Mazar (tomb) is situated. The Hazaribagh JPP outpost and earlier a Bush Police camps at Sonapahad restricted the movement of the Jarawas. To the north, a large settlement area is Ferrargunj which is adjoined by the both revenue and forest villages to northward such as Beachdera, Jhinganallah, Miletilak, Jirkatang No1 and Jirkatang No 2. These villages are highly interrupting the free movement of the Jarawas. On the other hand Jarawa police outposts were established at different sensitive points of the Jarawa appearance including the Hazaribagh JPP Outpost, JPP Outpost Miletilak and OP Jirkatang2. There were forest camps at Putatanag and Jirkatang No7 which later had to be dismantled.

The Beachdera, Jhinganallah and Jirkatang areas were majorly populated by the ranchi people while Miletilak was initially colonized by the Myanmarese and now dominated by the south indian families. These areas were under severe threat of the Jarawa attacks since their (settlers') settlements came into being. Recently the Jhinganallah people who were encroachers of the forest land have been evicted. During the year 2004 I was positioned at Middle Strait to handle the Jarawa situation from Jirkatang to Middle Strait and the adjoining areas. At Jirkatang No2 I was allotted one residential quarter in a school premises. There I enjoyed fresh water being supplied inside my quarter through the pipelines for 24 hours having the water source in the Jarawa area. The villagers of Jirkatang have raised their plantations near the Jarawa Reserve and they grew banana, tapioca, coconut, lemon and other fruit bearing trees. Some of the plantations are situated between Jirkatang No 02 and Jirkatang No 07. On 10-04-2006 morning, 8 Jarawas entered the plantation of Shri C. Moideen near Jirkatanag No 02 after crossing a nallah by swimming. Self with one assisting staff observed in the field that the Jarawas did not take anything from the plantations. Our investigation further revealed that they only extracted honey from the trees in the plantation area and now wanted to return back. We with help of the plantation owner somehow arranged a wooden raft and helped the Jarawas to leave the plantation by crossing the crocodile fetched nallah. These areas were frequently raided by the Jarawas mainly against the logging operation since the British period. There was a Bush Police camp at Bamboo Tikrey for protection of the forest workers. The pig and deer hunters are still using the Jarawa Reserve from distantly located villages such as Wrightmyo, Manarghat, ShoalBay 15, ShoalBay 18, ShoalBay 19 that are connected with Jirkatang and Miletilak (once Miletilak was a camp area of the natives) through creek. Near ShoalBay there is a tiny island called Kyd Island which was abode of one of the bands of the present Great Andamanese. It is mentioned in a report that the Kyd Island was occupied by Aka-bea group and their camp was called Duratang. Jatang, directly west from the Kyd Island was another camp site of the Aka bea group and the Jatang Hill was also used as a survey station during the British era (Temple 1923:59). During the punitive expeditions carried out by the British against the Jarawas in 1901 and 1902 expeditioners started from sites such as Jatang, Pochang and at Port Meadows on the east coast, in addition to some places on the west coast. The tiny islands such as Kyd Island, Port Meadows and Napier Bay situated between Shoal Bay creek and Putatang creek had been for a long time resource ground for the natives. But a former Bush Police camp at Port Meadows and other sensitive places of the Jarawa activities restricted the Jarawa movement in the region around Napier Bay, Kyd Island, Port Meadows and the entire creek. Here at this point of discussion I dont find any urguable reason behind why Kyd Island and other adjacent islands have been kept out of the reserve boundary. To this hunting-fishing ground the Jarawas quite often come from their traditional camp areas of Jatang, Pochang and Putatang. During my working in the year 2000, the Jarawas of Punanallah and Putatang jointly operated hunting expeditions in this area on several occassions.

In association with the construction of the Andaman Trunk Road there was notable for the Jarawas a large scale of timber extraction along the road. Forest camps established at various places including the Putatang region which was one of the major camping-hunting ground for the Andaman natives. In March 1996 a group of 60-70 Jarawas ambushed extraction workers from the Putatang camp killing two labourers and injuring three(Manish Chandi 2002). The Jarawas evidently always disliked the logging operation.

The Putatang forest camp was operational until 1996, after which only a few staffs were stationed to lookafter the things. Now there is nobody and only the remnant of the camp is seen. The Jarawas sometimes come to the Putatang camp site to collect mangoes from the trees grown by the dwellers of the forest camp now abondoned. There is flat land around the camp area wherein sometimes spotted deers and most of the time large number of stray cattles can be seen. These cattles were released by the Port Blair Municipal Council in 1998. If you make a travel from Jirkatang to Middle Strait through the Andaman Trunk Road, on several places on road mostly at Jirkatang No7 near a ruined forest check post and at Putatang you can see a hundred of stray cattles obstructing the vehicular flow; or we can say that those stray cattles were pushed into the Jarawa Reserve. It is high time to clearly understand that the Jarawa Reserve is not a 'Dumping Ground'or a cattle shed.

Further to the north, the Baratang Island I should essentially mention about. This island has become one of the major tourist destinations in the Andaman islands for its world famous Mud Volcanoe and the Limestone caves. In a particular season more than 70-80 vehicles every day reach here from the capital Port Blair with a large number of Indian and non-indian tourists. This island is geographically located between the South Andaman and the Middle Andaman being separated by the Amitla Boicha Passage from the South Andamans and Humfray Strait from the Middle Andaman Islands. The tourists intending to visit the Baratang Island are also shown the glimpse of the Jarawas by the tour operators while they are on the Andaman Trunk Road heading to-fro Baratang Island. The Baratng island was historically a land of Aka-Puckiwar tribe later on occupied by the Jarawas and now Ranchi people are settled on this island. At present this island is not inhabited by the tribes but once the island was taken as their own territory by them. The Talipot palm (c. umbraculifera linn) found abundantly in this island is called 'Barata' by the Andamanese. The Jeru group of the Great Andamanese say 'Pāroto' (explained by Andamanese chief Jirake during my working as i/c Great Andamnese settlement on the Strait Island). The Baratang Island and the surrounding area including the Flat Island in pre-1900 were occupied by the Jarawas. During his survey of the flora of the islands between 1913 and 1920, C.E.Parkinson (1972:268) came across an old Jarawa encampment in the midst of the palms on the Baratang Island. Probably with the gradual extinction of the Andamanese the Jarawas were occupying the island. Earlier the Bush Police placed their camps in different island pockets such as Lal Tikry, Nilambur, Wraftess Creek, Pawajig, Lorojig, Flat Bay, Bolcha, Papita Dera,

Bamboo nallah and South Creek etc. In the forest villages of Baratang in 2000 I counted there were 8 households in Nayadera, 15-20 in Mirchi Tikry, 10 in 3No Villar, 40 in Wraftess Creek, 40 in Khatta Khadi, 45 in Khatan, 54 in Jarawa Creek and around 50 in Baludera.The camps directly and indirectly interrupted the free movement and migration of the Jarawa from one place to another.

Moreover the Jarawas were restricted to somersault in their own courtyard. They were restricted to enjoy their own resources in and around the island due to increased activities of shark hunters, shell and swiflet nest collectors, fishermen, crocodile poachers, deer and pig hunters and the timber and bamboo smugglers. Even on the west coast the poachers come to collect the Flotsam such as plastic barrels, nets, ropes, dry bamboo, and wood and seasonally the umbergris. The forest on a large scale was extracted on this island and in place trees like Teak, Padauk and Pynma were grown up which have no use for the Jarawas. The Jarawas neither make their bow, arrow or anything nor fruits from these trees. In fact these trees are no more suitable to the natural ecological niche.

Now let us move to further north to discuss about the villages located within the domain of the Jarawas' hunting ground. The Kadamtala region is southern tip of the Middle Andaman comprising of some other villages of Bengali peoples. The name 'Kadamtala' derived from the presence of Kadam trees (*Anthocephalus cadamba*). Earlier the region was used for timber extraction to be transported to Long Island and Porlob Island. The old Ranchi people still do live in the old forest camps at Foster valley, McCarthy Valley and Boreham Valley on the eastern side. These areas are surrounded by the Boronjig, Porlobjig and Potijig. The residents of Kadamtala village, Uttara village and Shantanu village are highly indulged in fishing and hunting activities. Their over hunting and contributing to ecological changes have adversely affected the Jarawas' hunting-fishing activities. Earlier the large number of Bush Police camps highly disrupted the Jarawa movement. These villages alongwith Rangat and Bakultala are established by clearing of the forest which was a sole abode of the natives and allotted to the people. The old villagers still recollect the sighting of the Andaman tribes in those days. The settlers were not satisfied with the land the Government allotted to them. They started clearing of backyard forest and encroaching the land for plantation or converting into the paddy fields. Yet another village significantly I should mention about. This is Phooltala. This forest village is 13 kms away from the Uttara was priorly occupied by immigrants from the Bangladesh wherein I counted about 28 houses during my visit there in the year 2002. I had a several visits to this village after the Jarawas entered the houses and took with them their belongings such as tools and implements and other metal items, cooking vessels and cloth items etc. On all such occasions that I came across it was in my observation that the villagers say one thing and the Jarawa say absolutely different. I do remember one such occasion when a family lodged a complaint of looting by the Jarawa. They submitted a long list of belongings reported to be taken away by the Jarawas from their house. In that list few jewel items were also mentioned for want of compensation. Following an instruction from my office self officially visited his house and found that the family head was occupationally a hunter with a small paddy field. As whispered by few neighbours, there was no jewel item in the house. He was so poor that his wife had not more than 3-4 saaris in their old trunk. Through my long experience with the Jarawas I firmely believe that the Jarawas are more honest and reliable than the others. On further enquiry what a Jarawa said interpreted as, "when they came to our huts and steal our belongings in our absence, then we don't go anywhere to say this. We just punished them to teach a lesson that they should not come to our area and steal our food". The AAJVS team of

Kadamtala led by Anup Kumar Mondal, Tribal Welfare Officer on several occasions destroyed hunting traps of the poachers in the reserve. The Jarawas have also been guided to do that. On many occasions the Jarawas themselves removed the hunting traps of the poachers from their reserve and reported to the AAJVS team.

The villagers of Phooltala created great disterbances to the Jarawas since the establishment of the village. The Jarawas have semi-permanent camps at Dhaninallah and their one hutcamp called Uli- Chadda is situated very near to the ATR and approachable for the settlers of Phooltala. The Phooltala village area is to south adjoined by Kesri Dera and to north there was a Bush Poilce Camp at Yeratilajig No9 near a water source often used by the Jarawas. In this large region there are several mangrove creeks that have become a hopeful fishing ground for the villagers named as Kalu nallah, Mitha Nallah, Dhani Nallah and Kunju Nallah which fall into the Boroinjig creek near Porlob Island. There were several Bush Police camps inadvertently to irritate the Jarawas at Bamboo Tikry, Yeratilajig 10 and Yeratilajig 11 (also called Atarjig). Such police camps acted as 'camps for hunters' with active involvement of the police staffs and the villagers. A Jarawa man pointed out few police outposts established near to their water sources.

There is a distance of 12 kms from Porlobjig No3 to Porlobjig No15. The Porlobjig No15 is a settlement along the road side inhabited by the families of workers from Forest, APWD and Bush Police. Further the forest camps are located at Charlungta, Borniel and Tikka Dera. There is a distance of 14 kms between Borniel-7 and Phooltala while 18 kms from Phooltala to Tikka Dera. The OP Charlungta is situated at 2 kms distance from Kaushalya Nagar. With the increase in number of villagers and their plantation and the forest extraction continued to be even after 1960 (The settlement of Kaushalya Nagar came into existence in 1962 after clearing of forest), the Jarawa trend of raids changed and much of the raids aimed only to pluck banana from plantations, take away iron implements and kill animals if create problems or irritate. One of the Jarawa men stated that when the police (Bush Police) started killing them, they started avoiding skirmishes in fear of bullets and began to steal their belongings at night. The hunters of Kausalya Nagar and Shaktigarh mentioned about the Jarawa camps in the dense forest near Flat island and Mount Oldham. The Jarawas previously on many occasions had entered the Kaushalya Nagar and took with them iron items, clothes, and utensils and injured the animals on most of the occasions. Beyond the Kaushalya Nagar to north Shaktigarh is situated at 03 kms distance and at 2 kms distance the next settlement is Bakultala. Now it is very important for me to point out that the ATR from near Kaushalya Nagar is routing directly towards east through the Kalsi region for Rangat on east coast keeping a wide distance from the Jarawa Reserve. From Porlobjig No 03 to the Kaushalya Nagar the ATR either intrudes(?) into the Jarawa Reserve and in some places run close to the Jarawa Reserve. But if one intends to travel, he may surely find some normal roads and few narrow paths beyond Kaushalya Nagar to the Chainpur via Tugapur and other villages and hamlets.

The Kalsi village was one of the largest extraction camps with services of log trains in the Middle Andaman region. The villagers of Kalsi witessed and suffered from many Jarawa attacks even after the Bush Police personnel were camped at Kalsi 3,4,5, and 6. The old Bush Police patrol path now used by the hunters is connecting to many distantly located revenue and forest villages. These villages include Laukinallah near Billiground, Chainpur and Hanspuri. Latter two villages have always been highlighted whenever discussion held over demarcation of the 'Jarawa Reserve'. The Kalsi hunters used to reach Lamba Pahad (Mount William) and Melagar Boilyu in early period.

In March 1999, I visited the Government Primary School situated at Laukinallah of Middle Andaman. The school was then connected through a forest path with the Billiground on the ATR side. From the ATR to reach the school I had to walk for about 30 minutes on the mud and the knee high grasses which were filled with leeches. The students and teachers gave interesting accounts of the Jarawa sightings in their backyards. One day morning they found some rough sketches on outer wall of the school by a red stone undoubtedly done by some naughty Jarawas. But interestingly they never tried to harm anyone of the school.

The Bakultala, the Rangat, the Mayabunder (earlier named Bonnington), the Billiground, the Betapur and few other villages are situated out of the Jarawa Reserve now being commercially developed. Bonnington (present Mayabunder) and Webi were the old villages where Karens from Myanmar arrived in 1925. The old persons have still in their memory the Jarawa sighting in their backyard. These villages populated by different ethnic groups are forming a different human-ecological scenario in the Middle Andaman region. These advanced villages with the increasing population influx stand on east while the Jarawa Reserve falls on west side of a single landmass (Middle Andaman). In future this will surely pose a serious problem to the survival of the Jarawa community, I strongly predict. Now most intensively the encroachment activities of the settlers be checked. A Bush Police Outpost was established at Luis-Inlet Bay in 1957. The Luis-Inlet Bay has still the Jarawa Protection Post to inadvertently disrupt the Jarawa movement. The region in and around the Luis-Inlet Bay comprised of Wolaga Boilyu, Melagar Boilyu, Chainpur nallah and Hanspuri area has since the time memorial been the hunting fishing ground for the island aborigines.

In June 2004, I visited these areas of conflict alongwith Shri. S.A. Awaradi, the then Director of Tribal Welfare,

Andaman and Nicobar Administration. During our visit we had a tiresome but successful trekking even in the marsh towards the remote hamlets around the Chainpur and Hanspuri areas. We reached Mayabunder in the evening of 7 June 2004 and after the night halt in the APWD Guest House at Mayabunder we resumed our journey on the next day morning. On the way to Chainpur we had a tryst with the people of Tugapur village and Bojotta/ Pudumadurai village. They confirmed about the Jarawa sighting in their locality. We further found there a Gramin Road of 1.8 kms length between N.C.Hawladar's house and Police Camp at Chainpur constructed in May 2003. Since the road was totally muddy and it was nonstop raining we removed our shoes and started walking. There were around 60 houses in the Chainpur village. Further we visited the hamlets of Kukridabla and Pynmadabla. At Kukridabla we found 9-10 vacant houses while at Pynmadabla there were about 11 houses. Baludabra is a place on the eastern side of Hanspuri where the Jarawas quite often made their advent. But the Jarawas did not come at Gandhinagar, Kukridabla and Pynmadabla. Further we visited the Sippy Tekry where we observed that the Jarawa Reserve was demarcated in the creeks by mere erecting of mangrove poles (Khadi Balli) in the water. Only the heads of poles were visible out of the water. On many spots the forest staffs nodded to the points where once such poles were standing now absent perhaps removed by the poachers.

The 1979 Notification indicates that the Jarawa Reserve links Woluga Boilyu Creek with the northern tip of Hanspuri village and outskirt around south west and southern side keeping the same half a km distance from Hanspuri extending to the Bush Police camp No 32 facing the Luis-Inlet including entire Wolaga Boilyu, Melagar Boilyu and Mar Boilyu creeks. But, the Jarawas still do not know where their boundaries (as we demarcated) run from and where they go to end.

One can easily reach Luis-Inlet Bay from Chainpur village through the creek. The Jarawa Protection Police was re-established at Luis-Inlet Bay on 10-04-2000 with strength of one head constable and few constables. The Chainpur Nallah further meets Luis-Inlet (Lungrawath Boilyu) where there is village of less than 35 families. Towards north from Sippy Tikry we reached Khokdidabla also known as Ganesh Nagar. The villagers of SippyTikry reported that the Jarawa had taken with them household items such as dao(a traditional cutting implement), knife, cooking vessel, spade, axe etc but not often. Reportedly the SippyTikry derives its name from a kitchen midden belonging to the Akakede group of the Andamanese found next to the creek. Similarly in case of the name 'Khokdidabla' the Khokdi name derives from a species of edible fern which is found abundantly around the creek and used by the Bengali and Ranchi people as vegetables. This vegetable is called Khokdi Bhaji in common parlance. The Dabla means small hamlet. This village is recognized as Ganesh Nagar by the department of revenue. The entire Jarawa Reserve to north limits upto the Hanspuri village , where there are many encroached hamlets such as Baludabla on east of Hanspuri, Naya Kattai, Sundari Khadi, Badak khadi, Karanj Khadi and Farsa naali and many others which people named themselves. These people have good workable knowledge about the forest paths, resources and water bodies in the Jarawa area.

During our field visit we received reports that the Jarawas entered the settlements of Chainpur on 02-3-2000, Hanspuri on 10-03-2000, Bojotta on 07-04-2000 and 62 Jarawas into Sippy Tikry on 18-05-2000. Thus we see that how the Jarawas in a short period make intrusion into several villages one after another perhaps for reasons better known to them. Now we return back from the Hanspuri towards south but this time not through the villages and hamlets already mentioned. Alongwith the shore line we find at first the Mask Island on west of Hanspuri. The Mask Island is not a Jarawa Reserve but used as Hunters' Camp and standing closest to the northern limit of the Jarawa Reserve. Surprisingly, the Mask Island, the Kyd Island and many other islands which fall within the vicinity of the Jarawa movements are not notified as Jarawa Reserve. These hotspots since very beginning have been the ideal grounds for hunting and fishing for the natives. The hunters, fishers and shell collectors from Mayabunder and other parts come to the Mask island and stay for several days. From here moving to south we find Tuff Island, Luis-in-let Bay, Robert Bay and Pilot Bay. Further in south of the Robert Bay we find along the west coast the Hump Island and ahead Rocky Point, a rock base for swiflet nest collectors who collect large number of white edible nests of swiflets to sale out at a very high cost. Edible-nest Swiftlet (*Collocalia fuciphaga*), also called Andaman Grey-rumped Swiftlet and locally called 'Hawabill' inhabit rock caves near the shore. Edible-nest Swiftlets are small, dark brown, slightly fork-tailed birds. Only those nests which are 'white' and made purely or almost purely of saliva are the most prized. The nests are harvested by the local poachers from walls of the caves which are located abundantly in the Jarawa Reserve on the west coast and in some islands, islets and rocks. Towards south of the Rocky Point, the Flat Island is located where many foreign and local poachers have been killed by the Jarawas. Down to south Yadita is situated on west coast of the reserve. From this point if start walking to southern direction after hours we reach at south end of the Middle Andaman Island where at mouth of the island, a geographically turning point Lakera Lungta beyond Foul Bay is situated. The Spike Island is situated just opposite of the Lakera Lungta. Close to the Spike Island towards south there is a tiny island called Bluff Island. These two islands (Spike and Bluff) still do play vital roles in traditional movement of the Jarawa between South Andaman and Middle Andaman. These two islands act amidst the sea channel as halting station for Jarawas in course of their movement between south and middle Andaman through west coast. These hotspots in early period used as the ground for launching the contact expeditions conducted by the local administration. After all the Jarawas' coming into our friendly contact, some horticultural practices have been introduced to the Jarawas at Spike Island by growing of banana, pineapple etc. The AAJVS' efficient field functionaries conduct patrolling to these areas and implement the welfare schemes. Now heading to south we reach Northern tip of the Jarawa Reserve in the South Andaman through Cape Bluff region. To south lie the Breakfast Bay and then Bilap Bay creeks where punitive expeditions were conducted by British in 1901-02 (Temple, 1923). During the same period on the other side punitive expeditions were organized in Port Meadows region. Further to south an area called Port Campbell comprised of and adjoined by Montgomary, Petrie Island, Defence Island and Clyde Island with beach areas of Dalrymple and Blair beach used in 1942 for marine operations. A dutch submarine captained by McArthy the then Superintendant of Police was anchored here and the captain and his team reportedly trekked to Ferrargunj to gain intelligence on Japanese activities. In 1943 another party came to this area for similar nature of operation. The anchorage for this second vessel also was at Port Campbell (L.P.Mathur, 1985). This place was once used for establishing an Andaman Home for the Andaman aborigines. To south of this historical harbour area within the Jarawa area, Petrie Island and Montgomary are located closely. The Petrie Island is used as camping ground by fishermen, hunters, shell collectors and the swiflet nest collectors. The local people frequently come to this region even in rough weather in search of Ambergris. The Myanmarese and Thai poachers also use the place as their hideout. The local people refer to this place as to Hiran Tikry. I came across few of the Jarawas at Partamjig Creek and Ike Bay. There are various names given for various spots on west coast from Cape Barewell to Constance Bay such as Badabalu, Kurma Balu and Chota Balu. Several Jarawa huts can be seen here with little distance from the coast such as Tothavikiji chadda, Nono-Ugey chadda, Wey-shekyep chadda, Eno-chadda (near Palmer Point) and the chaddas of Tirur region. The Bengali settlers from Tirur and Wandoor largely gather at this area. On many occasions during my official visits I found several engine dinghies anchored for hours in the shallow water in the Badabalu area which is a major fishing ground for the Jarawas.

Thus the long discussed Jarawa Reserve at coast is stretched between Constance Bay on south and a place at Hanspuri of Middle Andaman on north through creeks, marsh, bays, rocks, tiny islands, hillocks, villages, forests and forest villages. But sadly no creek and no land point is free of poachers. Though the Jarawa do not know the art of canoe making they used rafts of bamboos, wood or Styrofoam pieces to cross the sea channels and creeks. Interestingly, the Jarawas have their own territorial systems and rules of them to follow honestly. The Jarawas of Middle Andaman region never came to the Tanmad area to occupy the territory and similarly the Jarawas of Tirur never made any attempt to occupy the land at Middle Andaman.

5

The Andaman Trunk Road

Earlier during the British period there was hardly 171 Kms of metalled road and that too around Port Blair. It is only after the project of rehabilitation of the displaced persons and repatriates the work of road construction was initiated. The road construction was done through the inaccessible dense forests of the Jarawas, the Onges and the Shompens. The issues concerning the Jarawa on the Andaman Trunk Road have seriously been discussed in all meetings, discussions and presentations but problems caused by the Andaman Trunk Road remain unsolved. Broadly there are two groups with different attitudes and opinions. On one side the experts and anthropologists advocate for closure of ATR with the remark that this road to an extent is a part of the Jarawa Reserve and is absolutely destructive to the Jarawas while the other group comprising of local people, contractors, traders and other people stand against closure of the ATR saying that the ATR is a life line for the island people. According to them this road plays a vital role in connecting the peoples in the isles. But why on the ground of snatching other's right? Why to make their courtyard our thoroughfare without having their permission? Gradually on the Andaman Trunk Road, the Jarawa Tourism has been developed and people are coming to see the Jarawas on ATR as if this is a Human National Park. Through the ATR, the natives are exposed to the modern civilization and its baneful influences like consumption of tobacco, zarda pan, alcohol, unfamiliar foods and diseases against which they have no indigenous immunity, which could together take them to the brink of extinction. I am no more hesitant to say that the Andaman Trunk Road called to be a lifeline for the settlers, in future may take the forest dwellers from one end to an end of 'END'.

The Jarawa Forest Area was declared Reserved Forest (RF) in 1957 by the then Chief Commissioner of the islands. There were settlements of different ethnic groups from Diglipur in the North Andaman to Port Blair in the south Andaman narrowly separated by sea. In order to build connectivity between these places the construction of the Andaman Grand Trunk Road was contemplated by the local administration during the second Five Year Plan and the work started in 1958. But at this point of time no effort was made to keep the reserve area out of the line or for de-reserving the Jarawa Reserve Forest area coming into the domain. For the construction of the ATR a large number of trees were chopped down. The Jarawas constantly protested through the showers of their sharp arrows. Several APWD workers e.g. Kalimuthu, Bhimbahadur (on 21-04-1969), Joseph Kujur, Emil Bara, Markose Tigga, Philmon Dungdung, Mangal Kujur and Budha Munda on 29-01-1971 and Dawood Kiro on 07-05-1972 were attacked by the Jarawas when they were engaged in construction of the ATR. Their attacks were so frequent and vehement that the work had to be transferred to Border Road Organisation (BRO). Being a part of military engineering they adopted orthodox method to combat the Jarawa menace. They erected fence of naked wire and electrically charged it at night. It was alleged that hundreds of the Jarawas electrocuted and died. But the Jarawas did not sit to take rest. The workers of GREF now required protection of the police against the Jarawa attacks. Many anthropologists, other experts and organizations from various parts had the common voice against the construction of the ATR. The construction of the present ATR started in 1973. After construction of about 87 Kms of the road the work was suspended in 1975 in accordance with the decision taken in a meeting jointly by representatives of Ministry of Home Affairs, Ministry of Shipping and Transport, Planning Commission and the Andaman and Nicobar Administration.. In a report it is also mentioned that the construction of ATR was in query by Indira Gandhi in 1980 on grounds of its running through the Jarawa Reserve. Later, an Environment Impact Assessment was taken up by the Centre for taxonomic studies, which clearly declared that the waterways should be used as a more viable alternative to the road, considering that the road was hindering the natural environment - the forest and its people, to a great extent. The position was reviewed in the 6th meeting of the Advisory Committee on Tribal Groups in Andaman and Nicobar Islands held on 9th December 1980 at New Delhi. Thereafter the work continued in 1984 aligning the road as far away as possible from the Jarawa reserve territory.

On the other side, SANE, along with Kalpavriksh and Bombay Natural History Society, had filed a case in the Kolkata High Court for the 'Restoration of the Onge habitat to the Onges. The case was referred to the Supreme Court and, while the facts regarding the survival of the Onges were being debated at in the court, the Jarawa case, i.e the negative impact of the ATR on the Jarawa livelihood was also brought forward, both cases being of the similar nature. The Shekhar Singh Commission appointed by the Supreme Court to study the forests and other allied matters in the Andaman and Nicobar Islands in 2002, later studied the ATR and its impact on the Jarawas in detail, with the assistance of the submissions made to the same on the basis of the studies conducted by SANE. The Supreme Court accepted the recommendation of the Shekhar Singh Commission's Report and passed a final order in favour of the closure of the ATR. The Supreme Court passed a surprising verdict by announcing the closure of Andaman Grand Trunk Road going through the the Jarawa reserve forest, i.e. from Miletilak to Middle Strait in south Andaman and from Purlobjig No 3 to Purlobjig No 15 in Middle Andaman within three months. The present Andaman Trunk Road stretching from the Chidiyatapu, the southern most point of the South Andaman to the Diglipur, northern part of the North Andaman connects north Andaman, Middle Andaman, Baratang and south Andaman at a length of about 333 Kms. Near 59 Kms of the road passes through the Jarawa Reserve.

Since the tribes have no linguistic link with the non tribal settlers, their violent reactions so far noticed may be construed as their message that they want to reserve the RESERVE in their favour. They expressed their unhappiness with the frequent poaching into their RESERVE by way of attacking on those who dared to enter, as revealed from their killings mostly within few kilometers from the villages in the reserve. I visited the place where kalimuthu was attacked and that was within 3 Kms from Jirkatanag No2. Shri Balakrishnan was also attacked near here. Kalimuthu who survived inspite of being hit by more than 20 arrows finally thanked to goddess Mariamman for saving his life and became priest for rest of his life. He constructed a Mariamman temple on a small hill at Jirkatang No 02 opposite Police Outpost. Such historical instances of Jarawa attacks becoming evidences reveal that they never wanted the construction of ATR and movement of outsiders through their patio. The available data reveal that the cases of Jarawa hostility from 1950's to 1970's were only around 75 in number while about 189 cases of Jarawa violence recorded in a single decade between 1980 and 1990 against the construction of Andaman Trunk Road, poaching and the activities of encroachment. The Jarawas apart from their attacks, found another way to protest against the road users. They would shoot arrows on the travelers going through the ATR. On 04-02-1995, one Shri B. Lachana got injury by a Jarawa arrow while traveling in a bus. On 01-08-1995 one girl was wounded by arrows shot on her while she was in a running bus.

After the Jarawas communally came out of their forest abode in broad day light for the first time in 1997, their appearances before the outsiders on the ATR increased. The Jarawas of the three main areas natively called Boiab (Tirur area), Thidong (Middle Strait area (Elentilipad) to south of Putatang area but before Tulichadda of Punanallah) and Tanmad (the west coast area including the Kekab (Kadamtala) area) began to construct many huts to stay on the ATR side preferably at Punanallah, Putatang, RK Nallah and Dhaninallah. The Jarawa of Boiab frequently came on the ATR and constructed huts at Billinallah, Punanallah and Putatang. As we like to build our houses on road side for want of facilities of the transport, they also constructed a large number of camp huts identified in peripheral forests near the ATR called Tulichadda, Bimuchadda, Tuichadda, wooley chadda (near phooltala), Lev chadda, Ulie Chadda, Alugithale chadda, Thapiem chadda, Alo-ethale chadda, Tahato and many others. Trying to board on a vehicle especially on tops of buses, street play and somersaulting by the Jarawa children on the ATR became usual scenario to view. Looking to the situation the AAJVS adopted new strategies to avoid Jarawa contact with the outsiders and prevent their intrusion into the settlement areas by deputing staffs at different areas viz. Kadamtala, Tirur and on ATR between Middle Strait and Jirkatang No02. Looking to the frequent appearance of the Jarawas on the ATR the tour operators started bringing the tourists to Baratang or other areas in north and Middle Andaman by road promising them to show them the glimpses of the Jarawas on the ATR. The Jarawa centered tourism has been increasingly in vogue on the ATR. They get Police permit to run their vehicles on the ATR in the Jarawa area on payment of certain fees. Accordingly TR5 (under Treasury Rule 83) is issued by the Police giving the details of the vehicles etc. In their journey of such untold JARAWA TOURISM the drivers pause their vehicle just near any Jarawa camp and request to the policemen to allow them to attend call of nature. They adopt another tactics as observed to become free of convoy and closely see the Jarawas on Andaman Trunk Road. The driver and tour operator stop the vehicle near Jarawa hut and immediately get down to check the tyre and sometimes show technical problems and in doing so they ably facilitate the tourists to have tryst with the Jarawas who come down to see what's happening. On 05/02/2002 I was on duty on ATR when an Omni got little slow and from its window few female tourists threw some pieces of ripped bananas at Punanallah before the Jarawas. The Jarawas stopped the vehicle from front and being quite dissatisfied to the distribution system, a Jarawa youth namely Gene accompanied by the other Jarawa members attacked with his dao on them. In effort to save the tourists I received a deep cut in my left thumb and it started bleeding. When Gene saw the drops of blood he and few other Jarawas rushed to a bush and brought few leaves and they did the same treatment as the Tirur Jarawa did to me on 24 November 2000 in a case of raid. To combat the situation the Andaman Administration has issued certain guidelines / instructions through Press Media and All India Radio (AIR) from time to time. The boards depicting Dos and Donts for the outsiders have been erected on various points where the movement of the travelers/ villagers and their possible contacts with the Jarawas have been identified/ notified. The CONVOY system has been introduced to prevent rough influx of the traffic and peoples on the ATR in the Jarawa Reserve between Jirkatang No 2 and Middle Strait in South Andaman and Purlobjig No 07 and Purlobjig No 15 in Middle Andaman. At various places alongwith the ATR in the Jarawa Reserve the auction board depicting 40 Kms speed for vehicles have been erected. The boards declaring NO OVERTAKING ZONE have also been erected on the road side of the ATR in the Jarawa Reserve. But the offenders do always find tiny holes in the existing system.

It is clearly indicated by the notifications even after the amendments that a long length of the ATR is either touching/ entering into the Jarawa Reserve or only for the namesake the road is keeping metres of gap which is undoubtedly badly affecting the 'Reserve- Rules'. The Andaman Trunk Road since its construction is highly obstructing the Jarawa access to some major creeks and waterbodies situated on the eastern sides. The Jarawas are usually seen crossing the ATR to reach these creeks and water bodies which are ideal grounds for hunting and fishing activities and particularly for crab hunting; but sometimes they are diverted by the outside movements on the ATR.

The ATR gradually became a ground for changes in the Jarawas' material need and for seeking modern mode of transportations such as vehicles to move from one place to another. For example 1) On 22/05/2002, 10 Jarawas appeared at Jirkatang2 to have vehicle to reach Tirur. But with painful efforts the functionaries of AAJVS successfully persuaded them to give up the idea of boarding the vehicle to reach their destination. Finally the Jarawas were agreed to go back to their place by walk and 2) On 29/09/2002 about 40 Jarawas for the very first time camped at Middle Strait jetty for want of a dinghy to go to Badabalu area (west coast). They constructed a temporary shed with leaves and began to prepare food near the jetty, the so sensitive non-Jarawa concentrated place. But with constant efforts for two consecutive days made by the AAJVS field functionaries, they successfully persuaded the Jarawas to go through the traditional route by walk to wherever they wanted to proceed. Finally The Jarawas went back to RK Nallah from where on the next day they proceeded to Badabalu by walk. The abve examples do not denote that the Jarawas are totally dependants on the vehicles running on the ATR for their transportation or the Jarawas have full will to camp on ATR side for all times. During the period of my work in the year 2003, I recorded in my diary, 64 days of complete absence of Jarawas on the ATR between Jirkatang and Middle Strait. At the time of the event of the earthquake followed by the great tsunami (Thopicha/Thumaithum) on 26 December 2004, there was no Jarawa on the said ATR portion. All of them were then camped at Badabalu (west coast). The ATR is not their old path, but it is mirrored that the black road is disturbing their normal living and movements.

The ATR acts as a way through the courtyard of the Jarawa area and the Jarawa children somersault on ATR to attract the outsiders and have a fun of contact. They beg for biscuit, chocolate, sweet items etc before the passengers as reactions to the habits of passengers who usually throw out eatables from windows for them whether asked or not. So such acts should not be construed as their 'begging in hunger'. The 'asking for food' by them is not new to us. The Jarawas when confined to their own forests searched pockets of the members of the administrative contact team in their contact expeditions. They asked for shirts and the things like sun glass, cap etc. The ATR passing through the JARAWA RESERVE caused several accidents injuring the Jarawas. A Jarawa girl namely Otalete was injured in a road accident and she was admitted in the GB Pant hospital at Port Blair on 17th June 2000. She was discharged on 7th July 2000. Tauthe has his hand fractured and bent, Gillet lost his hand, Othahene has his right leg bent and Athawa has got his left leg bent. On 11 Octobar 2002, A Jarawa boy named Raja of 13 years appeared as a witness and identified the errant driver in a Hit & Run case, in the court of Judicial Magistrate First Class II at Port Blair. He in fact has become the first ever person from the Jarawa community to do so. This boy of Lakeralungta virtually sprang a surprise to everyone with his determination and stead fastness as he kept calm and stood by his statement even in the midst of cross-examination in the court room. Raja was witness to a ghastly accident on ATR that took place one year ago, involved a speeding jeep that hit a Jarawa boy called Tahai. Thus the Jarawas were not hostile while the ATR of their courtyard became 'Hostile Road' to them. The movement of vehicles in convoys on the ATR has promoted gift economy among the Jarawas and limited their traditional movement affecting adversely their subsistence activities of hunting, fishing and collection.

The Administration of A & N Islands has been provided with a time frame to activate alternate means of transportation by building up a sufficient waterway infrastructure to function after the closure of certain ATR portion. Now the efforts may be made to have boats through the Shoal Bay creek to Baratang to avoid the use of ATR under the Jarawa Reserve between Jirkatang and Middle Strait and from Uttara to Yerreta Jetty to avoid the ATR under the Jarawa Reserve in the Middle Andaman. A proposal was also mooted to construct a new jetty at McCarthy Jetty in Shoal Bay about 20 Kms from the Bambooflat. The creek at McCarthy Jetty is quite wide and deep to harbour large vessels. The vehicle ferry would have a safe journey in sheltered waters of the creek except a brief exposure to the sea near Kyd Island before entering Middle Strait. During British period McCarthy Jetty was in frequent use and the officers used to sail from this jetty for surveillance and transportation. The jetty was then linked with a road. DAM McCarthy, Commandant and the then Superintendant of Police along with Captain Harvey, Engineer and Harbour master and three other British officers had made his final escape from this jetty in a vessel nemely MV Sohrab just before the Japanese landing in 1942. For the said reason the local settlers call this jetty as McCarthy Jetty and they use the jetty for fishing purposes.The administration engaged WAPCOS as consultatnts to find out the safer and shortest alternate sea route to Baratang to Port Blair. The glorious history of this jetty may come back soon.

People having different perceptions on closure of the Andaman Trunk Road can broadly be divided into two. People including anthropologists, sociologists, environmentalists and other experts advocating for closure of the Andaman Trunk Road are few in the islands while the people including tradesmen and large number of settlers of North Andaman, Middle Andaman and Baratang backed by few politicians are speaking against the closure of the road. The politicians speak about the plight of the villagers with no words on 'Right of the Land' for the Jarawas. Many of the people on finding of no words against the closure of the ATR advocate for resettlement of the Jarawas admitting that the tribals come to plunder bananas from their plantations. In my long duration of work in the Jarawas areas I found many settlers who live at one place and at some distance grow plantation in the Jarawa territory or near to it encroaching partially the Jarawa land. For example, Few settlers of Manpur village grew plantation at about 6 kms distance in the Jarawa area near Collinpur. But it is also true that the Jarawas come to the present settlement area and pluck fruits. But most of such areas were used by the Jarawas before the people began to live or raise plantation there. Now their coming out of the demarcated territory and plucking of fruits from the plantation is often termed as 'their raid' by the villagers and also in some administrative reports. We also use the word 'Raid' conventionally in our works. Such coming out of their forests (we demarcated not they) cannot be indicative that there is lack of food in their forests. In the two days' international seminar to draw policy on the Jarawa on 27-28 May 2004 most of the PRI members though demanded opening of ATR, failed to support their demand. Some of them assert in their political Bhaashan with no heed to the Jarawa welfare that the ATR should not be closed under any circumstances. One officer of the APWD argued that the closure of ATR would badly affect LPG distribution in the northern islands. I must gift him one copy of this book as token of 'Common Sense'. The people of islands like Neil, Havelock, Little Andaman and twelve islands of Nicobar district (after tsunami few depopulated) have no problem of LPG distribution. On the issues revolving around closure of ATR, I interacted with hundreds of settlers including the highly educated people and deplorably I found in them no sense of obligation towards the Jarawas. They should understand that the Jarawas are also the Indian citizens and we know what are our fundamental rights and the freedom of life. I interacted with many of the teachers and other government servants stationed at Baratang and northern parts who abscond themselves on every Saturday or holiday to visit Port Blair or other parts without having station leaving permission and return back to same station before office opens on next working day. They say that they would be in trouble if ATR is closed. Many people I met who said that after closure of the ATR they may not able to reach at time the other parts of the islands when needed. Surprisingly those people who said so never or occasionally came out of their villages. At Kadamtala many Bengali settlers used their tongues indecently in public meetings insisting to kill or shift the Jarawas to a separate place in the matter of closure of ATR. Many of them I noticed are poor vegetable vendors who grow vegetables on their small land in meager quantity. In addition to the vegetables they sale live country hens, eggs, loti (roots of an edible plant found abundantly in small water bodies) in either Panchayat market or on road side on ground carpeted by gunny bags. These people love to have tittle-tattle and never or very occasionally traveled through the ATR to visit Port Blair. Few people expressed their security concern stating that in case of any natural calamity or war the roadway is fastest mean of transportation. It may be mentioned to them that the road links especially the bridges are preferably targeted by the enemy side in a war. As the Navy and Coastguard proved themselves from time to time we should always keep trust in our Andaman and Nicobar Command components of all the three services viz. the Indian Army, the Indian Navy and the Indian Airforce with the Coast Guard component. The 'guardians of the sea' the Indian Coast Guard constituted on 1st February 1977 is effectively safeguarding the Exclusive Economic Zone (EEZ) around the islands which approximately constitutes 30% of the India's EEZ. Secondly in case of any natural calamity like earthquake and fire in forests, going through road amidst forest is more dangerous and risky than the sea journey. And most importantly, very rarely any ship meets with accident comparing to large number of major and minor road accidents in a year. Now one can easily understand which way is safe–sea or road?

In my memory there is a long list of tour operators who came forward to discuss about what will happen to them if ATR is closed. Certainly they shall be jobless but all tour operators have temporary jobs depending on the mercy of their masters. It is also obvious that there are lots of scope for employment in the sectors of fisheries (The Tuna fishing as 44% fishery potential of the fishery of the islands is only accidental and not targeted), inter-island private shipping, creek cruise through the mangrove creeks and tourism excluding the tribal areas and other sensitive parts of security concern. 'Tour to Andaman' is not a nightmare without JARAWA TOURISM.

The ATR is the only long road of the Andamans which runs through the South, the Middle and the North Andaman islands. Such a long stretch of the ATR if situation is not brought under control can soon be recognized as for our sadness the nation's only road for the Tribal Safari. As per a news dated June 16, 2010, some travel companies are running "human safari tours" to enable tourists to glimpse members of the Jarawa community. Survival International, which campaigns on behalf of the tribal groups worldwide, said it had found eight travel groups on India's tropical Andaman Islands promoting tours to see the indigenous Jarawa people. Four of the eight travel companies identified by Survival have since removed references to Jarawa tours on their websites, but four have persisted despite government warnings, it said. I must also join in this context that the London based Survival International is based at thousands of kilometer away from the Andamans but truly reported. Over here I personally know many tour operators who play several tactics to show Jarawas to their guests as part of their touring points and these clever tour operators are never caught by the web watchers and the local authority. Sometimes only the drivers do this job and owners remain mute and neutral on this issue for dubious reasons.

The overall situation is grim on the ATR. Tones of Bitumen are annually burnt to repair the ATR harming the ecological niche of the tribal reserve with help of firewood cut down from the forests usually go unchecked by the Police and Forest department. The coal fire emits large quantity of fly ash and Sulphur Dioxide. Fly ash is a major health hazard while Sulphur Dioxide causes serious respiratory ailments. The vehicles running on ATR produce Carbon Monoxide and lead, which are dangerous to the Jarawa health. The thick smokes omitted from the vehicles pollute the environment and choke for the time the breath of Jarawas standing on roadside. January 2003 was taken out as a sample month from the police record and as per the record 2815 vehicles in this month passed through ATR from Jirkatang to Middle

Strait. In the Jarawa Reserve the Andaman Trunk Road has become dumping ground of garbage consisting of polythene bags, plastic water bottles, empty beer and wine bottles sometime half consumed, snack packets, tins and other wastes thrown out from windows of the vehicles. The Jarawas have started using discarded and uncrushed plastic bottles collected from the road sides to store drinking water, honey, and the pig fat for making bow strips. They never wash the bottles once brought into use. These dirty bottles carry diseases unknown to the Jarawas. A plastic bottle is made of Lexan Polycarbonate resin. The plastic made from this can leach bisphenol –A (BPA) - a potent hormone disruptor. BPA- a harmful chemical can be leached into the water bottle's contents through normal wear and tear, exposure to heat and cleaning agents. There is always a kind of competition among the Jarawas in collecting eatables from the vehicles. But the Jar ıwas have their own system of social control. They pay respect to the senior members and they never fight for food. Now they collect eatables from the vehicles with full individual attempt to collect in quantity more than the others. They drag and push each other while collecting eatables. Now this very harmonious social value of the Jarawas is also in serious threat. The respect for each other may be obsolete in future.

Rupees in crores are invested in repair and maintenance of Andaman Trunk Road through out the year. The closing of ATR means saving of money in crores. The APWD workers in large numbers being unchecked daily make to-fro between their homes and the Jarawa reserve. Few Jarawa children always come to them and sit near to them to get their lunch wastes. Nobody is there to check the health status of the workers to assess how many of them suffer from contagious diseases. If such rough mingling of the ATR workers with the Jarawas continues then there may be more alien diseases added to already reported diseases and health problems such as RTI, URI, Pneumonia, PUO, Malaria, measles, mumps, unknown poisoning, tuberculosis, skin diseases, abdominal pain, ear and eye infections, and other diseases etc. thus making a long list of diseases in the medical sheets of the Jarawas.

Few APWD workers before start of the assigned work go to the thicket and pitch traps to hunt spotted deer and wild boar and check their traps whenever get chance. On finding any prey, they immediately remove and drag the unlucky animal to a water source and cut into pieces. The group who take part in the operation equally share and keep the venison/pork in their lunch boxes. The old clothes, pan, zarda and other strange items are often gifted to the Jarawa members by the workers. Sometimes wool, clothes, biscuits, used cap and garments, etc are offered to them for want of pig, crab, resin and mainly honey. This barter system is practiced not only by the APWD workers but also some truck drivers and tour operators who frequently travel. In the year 2001 a Jarawa boy fell from a tree and broke his back bone ultimately died despite all efforts of the government to save his life even by shifting to Chennai. This boy was in the habit of chewing tobacco. Because of the intake of tobacco and its intoxication he lost his balance and fell down from the tree and finally died. Apart from such cases few Jarawas became eulogists of some regular drivers, APWD workers, policemen and passengers. Apart from the AAJVS workers many APWD workers, drivers, cleaners and tour operators have also learnt to use some Jarawa words. Once a word came to my ear 'chaagi' means 'get down' spoke to a Jarawa boy by a truck driver when he (the boy) tried to board on his truck at Middle Strait. Few Jarawas have confessed that they consumed liquor also offered by them but emitted soon because of strange acidity in taste. This is good for all of us that the Jarawas communally are still not in grip of alcoholic temptation. As result of frequent contact, over exploitation of their resources and sometimes false promises given by the outsiders, the Jarawas have also come on the line to tackle them with some tactics. One day I was coming from Middle Strait by my official bike following a truck convoy of evening. Since I was riding behind the truck convoy nobody noticed me. When arrived near Putatang Jarawa camp, on a turn as it was a clear further vision to me from behind, I saw a truck suddenly got to be slow near Ledha, a Jarawa boy standing on roadside holding a polythene bag full of resin pieces. The driver being unaware of my presence on his back quickly threw a ten rupee currency note, received the resin bag from the boy and accelerated further. It happened within few seconds. When the truck passed out, the boy saw me and started madly laughing 'ho-ho-ho-ho' by holding his stomach. When his laugh subsided he explained that he sold out not the resin but white stones in the polythene bag. But every boy is not Ledha. Apparently the Jarawas are innocent but clever too. On the ATR, the AAJVS staffs and staffs of Jarawa Protection Police perform duties to prevent any unpleasant incident concerning the Jarawas. During the last week of March 2004 a policeman thrashed a Jarawa boy for reasons best known to him. Few days after the incident on April 4, 2004 a group of the Jarawa came out at Middle Strait and burnt the Police Out Post. This was a planned revenge by the Jarawas who though are not worldly wise but are wise enough to make people understand that they would not bend down to atrocities committed on them.

No doubt in saying that the Andaman Trunk Road is as observable provides smooth black surface to the vehicles to run on it but in other words is in a mad rush to transport the sane Jarawas from one end of their ancient civilization to the dusty world of crime, drugs, diseases, corruption and mockery wherein they are sure to find themselves on Road-Zoo as roaming heritage of the world's oldest homo sapiens.

A Port Blair lawyer Shyamali Ganguli filed a Writ Petition 048 of 1999(PIL) in the High Court Circuit Bench, Port Blair under article 226 of the constitution of India on 24th May 1999. In her said petition clearly, she was in favour of the resettlement of the Jarawas like that of the Andamanese and the Onge. She demanded for supply of food through the plantation of fruit bearing trees on ground of the ATR scenario. She was neither aware of the disastrous effects of "Resettlement" of the Onge and the Great Andamanese nor the adverse ecological effect of the plantation in a rain forest.

In the said case, the High Court of Calcutta (Circuit Bench at Port Blair) directed the Central Government as under:

> "The Central Government through the Principal Secretary, Ministry of Home Affairs, within two months from the communication of this order shall form a Committee of Expert with the Lt. Governor of the Islands as the convener, comprising of renowned anthropologists, sociologists, nutrition experts, doctors for immediately undertaking a scientific study, research and survey in the aforesaid change in the behaviour of the Jarawas and to find out the cause of the same....
>
> "The said committee shall submit its report within six months from the formulation of such committee before the Central Government and Lt. Governor, A&N Islands and also shall file a copy thereof before the Circuit Bench of this court.
>
> "Within six months thereafter the Central Government through the Home Secretary himself and the Lt. Governor of the Andaman and Nicobar Administration shall formulate a policy, plan and programmes on the aforesaid questions whether the steps should now be taken for bringing the Jarawas in the mainstream of the society or they should be left to their own way of life as before or the balance between the two should be struck following

the peaceful existence theory as suggested by Mr. Awaradi in his MasterPlan or any other experts. For the aforesaid purpose the Central Government shall arrange seminars and open discussions of the different experts, National and International on the line, Anthropologist, sociologist and others and also individuals and Non-Government Organisations having knowledge and experience in the matter inviting them by issuing public notification in widely circulated news papers and sending them letters of invitation and thereafter shall frame the policy decision within the stipulated period after deliberation and discussion on such opinions with the approval of the concerned Ministry. The Central Government shall also publish the papers, discussions and deliberation of such seminar, at its cost, for future reference...

"After formulation of such policy the same shall be notified by the Central Government and the A & N Administration and shall also be placed before the Circuit Bench of this Hon'ble Court for appropriate order".

Accordingly the Ministry of Home Affairs, Govt of India has constituted a committee of experts vide their Notification No U-14040/24/99-ANI dated 21-07-2001 The expert committee under the convenership of Hon'ble Lt. Governor, Andaman and Nicobar Islands has constituted multi-disciplinary teams to study various aspects of the Jarawa life. The members of the multi-disciplinary teams called as Composite Groups were representatives from the Anthropological Survey of India, Botanical Survey of India, Zoological Survey of India, RMRC, Directorate of Health Services, Department of Forest and the Nutritional experts.

Three Composite Groups at three Jarawa areas viz. Boiab (Tirur), Thidong (around Middle Strait) and Tanmad (West coast of Middle Andaman) conducted study of the various Jarawa aspects in three different phases (seasons) from 10th

December 2001 to 9th January 2002(First Phase), 12th April 2002 to 10th May 2002 (Second Phase) and 10th August 2002 to 9th September 2002 (Third Phase).

The Committee of Experts submitted its report before the Hon'ble High Court of Calcu tta on 28-07-2003. The Central Government organized two seminars one at Kolkata on 7-8 April 2004 and another at Port Blair on 27-28 May 2004 wherein experts, NGOs and individuals deliberated on various issues relating to the Jarawas and their well being. Yet another study report has been submitted by the Sub-Group of Experts led by Prof Syeda Hameed, Member of Planning Commission, New Delhi on the Jarawa issues in 2006. She visited the islands on 12th May 2006. The said Sub-Group of Experts submitted principal recommendation for creation of Jarawa Tribal Development Authority (JTDA) for special protection and welfare of the Jarawas. Though many of the experts including those who are concerned with the Survival-International Charitable Trust, a UK based NGO, George Weber's Andaman.org, SANE, a local NGO, Kalpavrikhsha, a Pune-based NGO and many others like Thomas N. Headland from the University of Texas at Arlington very occasionally and few of them never visited the Jarawa areas, they rightly understood the crux of the situation concerning the Jarawas and caught the pulse of the Jarawa problems. Their documentations and recommendations sit fit to our (field functionaries) understanding and urge. These thinkers through their interpretations/presentations have expressed their deep sense of love and care for the vulnerable Jarawa. The UK-based 'Survival-International' situated at thousands of kilometer away from the islands continues its high profile efforts to protect the rights of the Jarawa. They have collected more than 46000 signatures from people all over the world. The people from more than 60 countries through this reputed organization have expressed their concerns for the rights of the Jarawas of the Andaman islands, from the Andaman islands themselves to the Arctic. But most of the local settlers to avoid the tension of 'CLOSING ATR' or to shift the onus on the ATR issue now talk about the resettlement of the semi-nomad Jarawa. To join the local lawyer Smti Shyamali Ganguli, they say in the same voice that the Jarawas should be resettled on a separate island with all infrastructural facilities to be given. Does it mean that their traditional movement in groups should be stopped or should be adversely affected? Or does it mean that they should be purely dependant on the government's free ration and other dole items for their livelihood like that of the Onges and Great Andamanese? In my opinion which I already expressed in the National Seminar on "Socio-Economic Changes in Andaman and Nicobar Islands Since Independence" held on 5-6 Dec 2002 organised by the Anthopological Survey of India, Port Blair through my paper on "The Policy, Approach and the Jarawa Volunteriness":

a. that when the Jarawas are settled at one place, the surrounding area is rapidly over hunted. They must go further and further for fishing and gathering to return with empty hands on most of the occasions. The result is a significant drop in protein intake, starting usually within a year or so. Further, being a lazy community they shall be depending on the dole items of the local administration.

b. that epidemics can wipe out almost the entire tribe if they are resettled at one place. When one member gets any contagious disease then others may rapidly come into its effect. For example, when the Brazilian government's National Indian Foundation (FUNAI) first contacted the isolated and nomadic Matis from Javari valley in Brazil in 1978, they numbered around 150. About 50% of the total population died following the first direct contact. After a series of epidemics including an influenza epidemic in which 53 Matis died, they were transferred to an area near a Government run health centre and away from the non-indigenous population. This seemed to be a very good decision. But since their transference, despite improved health care, Matis have continued to live in depression. Similarly as per a report the approximately 600 Panara from Brazil were first contacted by the outsiders in 1972. This led to an epidemic of influenza with massive mortality in the tribe. 186 Panara died in the first two years. Thus they were transferred to the Xingu Reserve in 1975. Many more died leaving only 69 survivors. The Panara complain that the Xingu Park is an "impoverished version" of their natural habitat. Finally the Panara have since returned to their own land and the Brazilian state has been found guilty of "causing death and cultural harm" to the Panara Indians by a federal judge (Inspiring report from Survival-International, London).

c. that the re-settlement of the Jarawas would lead to a catastrophe from which the Jarawa would be unlikely to recover. It may be worthy of note that a similar experiment with other tribes of the islands viz. the Great Andamanese and the Onge ultimately led to the drastic reduction in their number. Now, in their new settlements they are gradually being free of all their indigenous socio-ecological values and cultural practices and are struggling to survive in small see-saw population.

When we study all the variables or the development programmes that directly and indirectly affected the negrito tribes Onge and Great Andamanese, we broadly find that it was the scheme of 'resettlement' that played lead role in the permanent distruction of the age old tribal communities. Of course it was better than the Elwin's concept of national park of the tribals and better than the idea of 'total isolationism' or the thought of segregation but we cannot say that the scheme of resettlement was a good result oozed out after a long time churning in the 'thinktank'. An effort to resettle the Jarawa may cause the permanent distruction of their environment and the biggest cultural shock. There may be human influences from outside the group further leading to the loss of identity. Above all we should always remember that the conditions under which they lived for greater part of their existence should not be destroyed.

The most important ground for all our arguments against the re-settlement of the Jarawa is our realization of the grave mistake after the re-settlement of the Onge at Dugong Creek in 1976-77 and in South Bay around 1980 and the Great Andamanese on Strait Island in 1969. Myself worked among both the tribes as Settlement in-Charge and closely observed the destructive result of the resettlement of the Andaman foragers.

During my period of work as Settlement in-charge of the Onge settlement in 2006-10, I observed that the Onges who are resettled have no habit of using Latrines. They are reluctant to clean them.Their defecation every day in a limited area in and around the settlement invites various types of insects and fly which cause sickness of the tribals mainly with intestinal parasites and disorders, dysentery and diarrhoea. Secondly I observed that they continuosly wear clothes because of the outsiders' frequent visits but do not wash them regularly. These dirty clothes cause fungal skin infections and many other diseases among them. They are dependant on the Settement in-charges (they call 'Entthale') for their social control, food and daily needs. The young members have scanty knowledge about their own herbal medicines and the art of canoe making. They are missing hearing from their grandparents. They do not try to learn from their old members how to make a thatched Beyra (Community hut) or Korale (individual hut). The very similar scenario I observed in the Great Andamanese settlement during my working period. In their marriages dal, rice, and spicy Indian dishes are offered as feasts in place of pork and turtle. Out of their 12 indegenous groups (septs) only three or four are presently surviving. Their songs have got a strange rhythm and their dance has got a new castume. The *Loss of Land, Population, Identity and Confidence* are the underlined result of the re-settlement of the Andaman Negrito. We recorded their numbers dwindled after re-settlement not only in the case of Onge and Great Andamanese but in all known cases of the re-settlement of nomads.

Socio-ecologically the Jarawas move in forests in different sub-groups from few major groups of the territories such as the Boiab(Tirur), the Tanmad (the area at Middle Andaman), the Kewkab (Middle Andaman area) and the Thidong (Middle Strait area) etc. When members of one group make a long journey and join any other territorial group, they are offered pork and fruits which enables the tired traveled group to take rest without their worry about hunting or fishing for food for that time being. The terrestrial groups of the Jarawas are in matrimonial relationships. In case of the resettlement their harmonious world will immediately be destroyed. If their members go to forest at a distance then nobody shall be there to give them water, food and shelter. The poachers shall undoubtedly occupy their core areas. Thus, the said facts reveal that the Jarawas who have no tradition of living in permanent dwellings if resettled are sure to find them cramped and very uncomfortable and the new things may permanently harm them. Of course the Jarawa voluntariness in contacting the people, and adopting of new health practices such as use of soap, hair oil and bathing etc are being observed but these do not express their high communal concern about their future and their mainstream will to change the indigenous life-style. At this stage when their free and uniformed consent can apparently not be obtained their re-settlement would constitute a violation of their human rights. A forced resettlement of the Jarawa can provide a fatal blow to the Jarawa and what may appear to the planners as a minor impact. Further such resettlement apart from anything else may also create legal problems, as India is a signatory of the International Labour Organisation Convention. 107 and Article 11 of the said Convention acknowledges the right of ownership, collective or individual, of the members of the populations concerned over the lands which these populations traditionally occupy shall be recognized, and Article 12 of the said Convention provides the populations concerned shall not be removed without their free consent from their traditional territories. Of course there would be a violation of the United Nations Universal Declaration of Human Rights if force is used for removing of the indigenous Jarawa from their land and way of life.

I interacted with some adult Jarawa members on different occasions in different circumstances as noted in my diary namely Enetha on 1-10-2005, Angethai on 18-09-2005, Tangna on 27-10-2005, Thodova on 29-05-2006, Napoji and Totopal (wife of Napoji) on 23-08-2006, and other Jarawas to know whether they would like to stay at one place? They replied - 'Nadem' means 'NO'.

The Jarawas have always loved to live in their forest abode. Even today when on one side their behavioural change, the frequent constacts with the outsiders and their impacts are observable right on the other side they do not like the poachers and the forest department to stay and work in their forests. On 22-02-2006 I alongwith one AAJVS staff Shri Balram Yadav visited the coupe area of Andaman & Nicobar Islands Forests and Plantation Development Corporation (ANIFPDC) at Beachdera, South Andaman and accompanied the workers till they completed their harvesting and elephantry works and returned back. The Jarawas on that day were not sighted but they were frequently sighted as reported by the workers. It was apparent from my enquiry that they on most of the occasions just came with the purpose to check the work and ensure that they (the workers) do not expand the clearing of forests.

The pressure of poaching activities is a problem which has thousands of legs and hands. The settlers' interference and poaching activities are increasing and multiplying. On the other hand the Myanmarese and Thai poachers who intrude with modern guns have no challenger from the front. There are many widows whose life partners have been killed by the foreign poachers. I experienced in the context of the contact between the poachers and the Jarawas that generally there is a bit difference between these two poaching groups. The local poachers try to make the natives their friends. They (local poachers) sometimes fix the day, time and place to contact the Jarawas; while the foreign poachers do their work in the forest and after few days or months return back to their place by their own boat. In their movement if they see any Jarawa man they do not hesitate to kill him. Now the poachers if apprehended are booked under the PAT regulation which has recently been amended to give enhanced punishment to offenders. The earlier punishment under PAT Act was one year's punishment or fine and offenders were getting away by paying fines only. Now as per the amended regulations imprisonment is mandatory and may extend upto 2 two years with fine. Offenders caught poaching in the Jarawa Reserve now have to spend time in jail on conviction. The offenders are likely to be booked under relevant sections of the SC/ST Act also, wherever applicable, when they are found harassing Jarawas. This is a non-bailable act. In June 2006, six poachers namely Dhananjay Mondal, Sachin Mondal, Arun Mondal, Sameer Chakraborty, Viswajit Roy and Sadanando Mondal who belong to Wandoor, were caught poaching in the Badabalu (west coast) where they were accosted by a Jarawa boy named Uligard. They beat the Jarawa boy and threatened him, and have been arrested under the PAT regulations.

6

The Route of Migration

During my work period their seasonal migration and the routes of their movement closely observed. I observed that the Jarawas through out the year seasonally (The seasonal months they refer to as Maya, Todala, Thada etc.) move from one place to another in order to collect seasonal food and water depending upon their availability at one place, to hunt, for fishing, to collect forest materials to make bow, arrow and containers and to meet their kins, etc. Sometimes, they change their forest track or postpond/prepond their journey in accordance with the rain (Voaleya), summer (Thomutua) and winter/cool (Anyame) which is generally absent, but when the body gets cool, they discontinue their journey. It is also noticed that they prefer to halt near a stream (Inkaw). There are certain customs governing the rights of a territorial group over its territory. Persons are free to forage within their own territory, but generally they on their honesty guidelines fixed by the community do not enter the territory of other groups. But the social interactions always take place between all the territorial divisions through marriages and social visits. Most members are related to each other through consanguineal or affinal relations. The Jarawas are very good swimmers. They come across the creeks in the Jarawa area between South Andaman and Middle Andaman not only to enter the settlement areas but in course of their economic activity and in movement from one habitat to another. It is noteworthy that the Jarawa do not reside at a place permanently. Their movement from one place to another place has one important reason and that is their kinship or friendship with other groups, but their economic purpose often becomes the basis. As far as the Jarawa movement from one island to another island is concerned, generally they swim across the creek mainly during low tide. They do not know the art of canoe making but I have seen simple water rafts they used to cross the creek and narrow channels with their kids and old members. Mainly they have two traditional ways of inter-island migration. The first is along with Middle Andaman. They perform journey between South Andaman and Middle Andaman via Spike-2 Island and Bluff Island by swimming mainly during low tide. The Jarawas take rest or camp temporarily on these said tiny islands. This region of Jarawa swimming has many tiny islands around the Spike-2 Island. These islands are Bingham Island, Bluff Island, Mangrove Island, Stoat Island and Talabaicha (talakaicha) Island Sanctuaries. Further to the north in Middle Andaman, the Jarawas are living in hutments scattered in the north- west coast of Roberts' Bay situated just opposite of JPP Luis-in-Let-Bay. The Jarawas in low tide after crossing the creek by swimming enter into the settlements like Hanspuri, Bojotta and Chainpur. The second major route of migration is between Baratang Island and South Andaman. Through this way they reach from one island to another by swimming. While passing by swimming they take refuge on LalTikrey called "Vaada" in Jarawa language, which is located near Wraftess Creek between Baratang and South Andaman. In the said second route of Jarawa movement the Jarawa usually come from South Andaman to reach some non-tribal settlements of Baratang. These settlements are Naya dera, Mirchi Tikrey, 3 No. Vilar, Wraftess Creek, Khatta Khadi, Katan, Jarawa Creek and Baludera etc. There are more than 200 households in these settlements. The people of these settlements have experienced Jarawa attacks on several occasions. On most of the occasions the Jarawas have plundered their plantation and took away the iron pieces, metal objects, vessels, cloths and other items of their need. Such looting activity is termed as 'huiege'or'hanichei' in the Jarawa language. Their senior members often lead journey through creeks and channels. The old members and persons having infants get support of thermocol/styrofoam pieces or small rafts to cross the creeks. Before crossing the creek they beat the water with wooden logs to drive away the crocodiles. But now a days the young kids do not follow the safeguard measures their elders tought them to cross the creek/small water channels. They without trying to ensure that the water is free of croc hurrily jump into the water and swim to reach the other end. I still remember one incident in which a Jarawa boy was killed by a crocodile while crossing the creek by swimming. It was December 2005 when information received that a crocodile killed a Jarawa boy on around 2nd November 2005 at Tirur area from:

1. A letter from Samir Acharya, Society for Andaman and Nicobar Ecology (SANE), Port Blair dated 08-12-2005 addressed to K.S.Singh, Dy. Commissioner, Andamans.

2. A news broadcasted by the AIR, Port Blair on 13-12-2005.

3. News published in the *Light of Andamans* on 19-12-2005.

After that with reference to the letter No 11-9/ AAJVS/ 2000/396 dated 19/12/2005 from the Executive Secretary,

AAJVS regarding killing of the Jarawa boy by a crocodile while crossing the creek in Tirur, I conducted an enquiry. At the outset the parents of the Jarawa boy (Father Thagawaye M 35 and Mother Thati F 30) who then admitted in the Special Ward of the GB Pant Hospital, Port Blair were interrogated in a sensitized manner. A Jarawa youth namely Homounda was also present there. They provided the following information.

- A Jarawa boy namely Tawai Tepohane aged about 8 years was killed by a ferocious crocodile while crossing a creek passage at Tirur near the old JPP Out post No 4 which has been devastated by the tsunami.
- The incident was occurred during the first week of November 2005.
- When the crocodile attacked on the boy, he was accompanied by the following Jarawa members.

i) Illy M 15

ii) Ukoya M 16

iii) Bonamaye M15

iv) Kunu M15 and

v) Acheyane M12

In the Outpost JPP Tirur the Police personnel including the In- charges of JPP and OP stated that they came to know about the incident only after the news broadcasted by the All India Radio on 13-12-2005. They said they were unaware of the incident. In this case the Jarawas were swimming towards the village area. The said incident was happened just about a half Km distance from the JPP Outpost No 4 and surprisingly even after they came to know about the case happened they did not go for a preliminary enquiry.

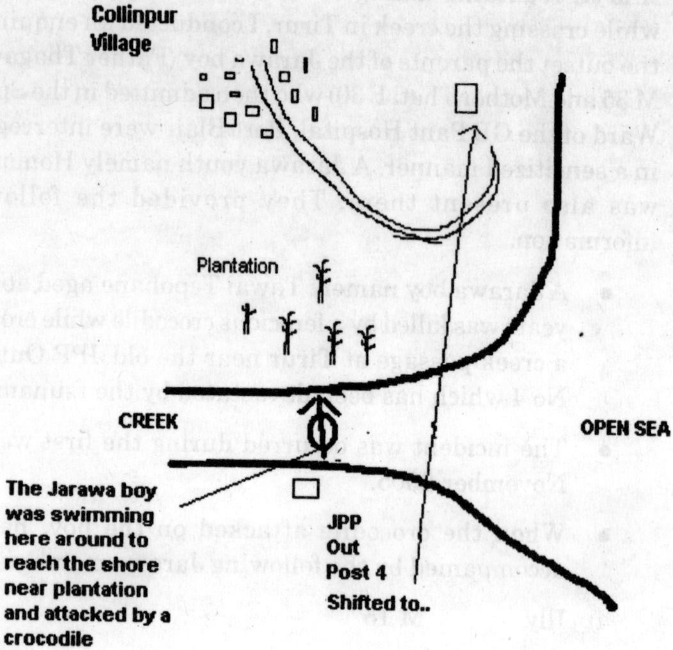

The people of Collinpur, the village located near to the incident area were well aware of the incident and those who came in my contact said 'yes, a Jarawa was killed by a crocodile'. But when insisted whether they witnessed or who witnessed they remained tight lipped. Some of them said that they came to know in November 2005. On an enquiry from the villagers, they said in low voice that few persons from the village end coerced the Jarawa boy to come by swimming their end just before being attacked by a crocodile. The people of the Herbertabad village informed in low voice that they came to know about the incident during first week of November 2005 when one policeman came to a tea stall at Herbertabad junction and in the midst of the gossip he told about the incident in front of many residents. But when the

Police further at higher level investigated into the matter nobody came forward to speakup.

Self on 21/12/05 wanted to visit the spot and meet the Jarawa boys Illy, Ukoya, Bonamaye, Kunu and Acheyane who accompanied the ill-fated boy while swimming but I had to delay my visit due to the lack of fuel in the police boat. On next day i.e. 22/12/05 after arrangement of little fuel for the boat self visited the spot of the incident as detailed by the Jarawas in GB Pant Hospital, the JPP outposts and the possible areas of Jarawa camping. From there around to Jhaukona area the Jarawas not found (or driven away?).

Thus through this sadful event exampled we noticed how the Jarawa movements are disrupted and the Jarawas are prompted to change their traditional paths. The geographical locations of the JPP outsposts and settlements and unsensitized activities and movements of the staffs and the settlers barricade the traditional routes of the Jarawa movements.

The plantations of the villagers near the Jarawa Reserve always attracted them to come there. On 20-02- 2006 to a coconut plantation near Collinpur, so called owned by Shri T.S.Vetaiyar S/o Shri Chinaperian R/o Temple Myo, few Jarawas came and made few temporary huts and camped therein at night. On the next day morning they left the place. Shri. T.S.Vetaiyar in his letter addressed to the Director (TW), A&N Administration stated that about 150 coconuts were plucked by the Jarawas from his plantation. On official instruction from the Executive Secretary, AAJVS vide letter No11-12/AAJVS/TW/01/567 dated 28th February 2006, self on 17th March 2006 visited the spot and interrogated with the Police personnel of JPP NO 04, Tirur and Shri. T.S.Vetaiyar and assessed the situation and noted succinctly but enough to conclude that 1) The location of the encroached plantation was situated near the Jarawa Reserve, 2) Shri T.S.Vetaiyar reported to the Director (Tribal Welfare) about

150 coconuts stolen by the Jarawas while he stated before me about 1000 coconut, quite contradictary.

In addition to the adjacent plantation, the adjacent small and big shops with hanging strips of tobacco and Gutkha pouches and chocolates in the jars at the village points and on road sides always attracted the Jarawas. They on many occasions instead of going through the heart of the forest went through such spots. For example, there was a canteen at Middle Strait which attracted the Jarawas to come there to contact the people for want of biscuit and snacks. While working in the area I closely observed a sudden increase in the Jarawa appearances at Middle Strait for want of biscuits and snacks. When the Jarawas appeared at this spot the people themselves came ahead to offer them pan and food items. As a result of special effort of the authority the canteen finally had to be closed.

It may importantly be noted that the Jarawas never used ATR as their route of movment before established friendly contact with the people. Now they use tops of vehicles to reach from one end to another. On several occasions the AAJVS hired vehicles and police trucks were also used to shift the Jarawas from one camp to another.On many occasions the villagers stopped field functionaries to bring the Jarawas to the camp located near their village. In May 2006, when about 45 Jarawas were dropped at Tirur near their reserve, the villagers stopped the police truck and did not allow the Jarawas to get down. They commented, "The staffs to control the Jarawas are appointed from far off places to work at Tirur. They never turn up and yet get paid. Why not appoint unemployed boys from the same Panchayat? We too can keep a watch on them". "Why bananas are not purchasd from our people?", the Pradhan further insisted. Traditionally the Jarawas have their own forest path between Tirur and Punanallah old Guest House, but the frequency of use of the old paths has been interrupted by the introduction of vehicles.

7

The Changing Behaviour and Outside Contact

Today one of the main subject issues of our study is the change in the behavioural pattern of the Jarawas as result of the frequent contact with the outsiders. The Jarawas themselves come out of forests and contact the outsiders at junctions, outskirt of villages and on road to meet their demands. They come to the junctions and road at Tirur with bags full of mud crab seeking pan or sukha (tobacco) or anything. They say in broken Hindi - kuch bhi chalega (anything can be given). The Jarawas are under increasing tactical pressure of the local poachers. Reportedly the villagers of Tirur and Collinpur kept the Jarawas under slavery. They engaged them in household works and in lieu of wage gave rice and sukha.

The poachers in such contacts always keep with them what the Jarawas do like most such as Sukha pouch (tobacco), biscuits, pan (bettle leaves) and rice etc. While all attention is on the Andaman Trunk Road some of the people particularly boatmen from Wandoor and other parts gradually started operating JARAWA TOURISM at remote parts on the west coast in the reserve. In such Jarawa Tourism the local poachers and tour operators are facilitating not only the local tourists but also the foreigners. They take them to the Jarawa territory to earn huge profits from the tourists. In 2008, the then Deputy Superintendent of Police (Middle Andaman) took personal interest to register a case against a local car which carried a tourist from Tamilnadu to the Jarawa area and the driver facilitated him in contacting the Jarawas and taking photographs with him. The tourist after return to home posted the photographs on the web site.www.exploreindiainfo.com. This serves the example that the officials are still doing something but there are difficulties in tackling the situation both individually and institutionally. There are many other recorded incidents in the recent years in which the foreign tourists entered the Jarawa territory with help of local poachers and did all the things on basis of–Give tobacco, rice and Rum and have Fun".

A French team of tourists led by Le-Figaro from Paris in 2000 entered the Jarawa Reserve and stayed for many days with them(Jarawas). They reportedly had sex with the Jarawa women. Similarly, Thierry Falise, a photo-journalist of international repute had stayed with the Jarawas for many days in January 2005 and later published a full blown article with attractive photographs in the Bangkok Post. The photographs he sold through a website name of which I should not mention here purposely. In the Bangkok Post dated February 21, 2005, Thierry Falise wrote " We are in forbidden water in the so-called "Jarawa Tribal Reserve" that streches along the west coast of the Andaman islands. These are also strategic waters. Further north, on an island in the Burmese Coco Island archipelago, the Chinese set up a naval base...Only daring people such as Jual come here. They run the risk of being arrested by Indian police or army patrols. But these forbidden waters are Jual's livelihood. He is an expert poacher and this is his hunting ground". Thus the Bangkok based photojournalist admitted daringly and proudly that he entered the Jarawa Reserve illegally with help of a local poacher. But the matter does not end here. He further disclosed the whole story of his visit in the section of *'Bangkok Post'* to give shock to the island administration for the first time brought into the notice of us through the esteemed local weekly 'The Light of Andamans' in its issue on 29th April 2006. The photojournalist made a trip to the west coast accompanied by two local poachers namely Jual and Rashid. The poachers facilitated him in all respects in his venture. They entered the Jarawa Reserve and received the welcome gestures from the Jarawas after the natives received a plenty of gift items from the visitors such as rice, bananas, pots, clothes and knife etc. Even after going through the caution boards indicating 'Dos' and 'Don'ts' on the Andaman Trunk Road, the photojournalist darely did all the 'Don'ts'. He commented that all these are meant for the islanders only. For many days they stayed with the Jarawas and remained hidden from the eyes of the forest and Police patrolling parties. It has been clear in the case of Thierry Falise that in the network of promoting Jarawa Tourism not only the persons like Jual and Rashid play key roles but there are many other persons who back them. Had Thiery Falise and Le Figaro no contagious diseases in them?

The cases of poaching in the Jarawa reserve by the foreigners like Thierry falise and Le-Figaro have shown the blackholes in our system. These have uprooted the fact that the initial result of the 'Outside Contact' has been geared up and multiplied leading to a complex situation which demands that we from time to time should closely observe and check the movement and activities of the tour operators and their vehicles, local boatmen and fishermen. The lodges, hotels and resorts may be the ground for such observations. We must not avoid the concrete fact that a strong network and mechanism has been built around to throw dust in the eyes of the administration. The chain of serious threats to the existence of the Jarawas hampering their all aspects of lives is not collectively one field to think over. In the administrative mechanism too we need to be more and more sensitized. Here "WE" means all of us including the Departments of Health, Forests & Environment, Tribal Welfare, Police, all Survey departments, and the Andaman and Nicobar Command from top to bottom should be more cautious, more actively responsible, and sensitized. The fishermen and shore poachers enter the shore areas of the reserve to fish and to collect flotsam such as plastic barrels, nets, ropes and occasionally ambergris that float ashore provide quick sources of income to them. They also collect commercial sea shells and edible nests of swiflet birds which go on high costs in the international market. Particularly I observed that the poachers mostly from Wandoor and Junglighat seasonally enter the stone caves on the west coast (Badabalu) to collect the white nests. The pressure on the innocent Jarawas is not from one end. On the other end the forest poachers enter the reserve to collect timbers of commercial values, bamboo, honey, resin and hunt spotted deer, birds and pigs.

Unfortunately the Jarawas themselves become shield in protecting them when a case is registered against a poacher friend of Jarawa. Their aggressiveness of the historical period has now turned to be flexible. In the journey from Past to Present they have been gradually devoid of the root trend to protect their women through their bows and arrows. There is not a far gap between a tribal expert and a poacher in understanding the changing behaviour of the Jarawa. The poacher who helped La-Figaro was well aware of the Jarawa behaviour. Similarly the poachers Haren Mazumdar, Narayan Roy, Dinesh Biswas, Ramdas and Rajesh Das and like them many others do know this changing trend of the Jarawas. At Ghaskhadi (Inechada) in Tirur in August-Sept (?) 2008 few Jarawa male members Annahmalai and others made complaint that few villagers camped with them for about a week and offered them IMFL and sexually harassed the women. The Jarawa complainants presented themselves before the Deputy Superintendant of Police and the Executive Secretary, AAJVS as witnesses. They admitted that five villagers later identified as Haren Mazumdar, Narayan Roy, Dinesh Biswas, Ramdas and Rajesh Das of Tirur entered the Jarawa territory and daringly stayed with them in Jarawa camp and reportedly the villagers shared with them liquor, rice and dal. When the male members went to hunt, they sexually exploited their female members. Against their history, this time their bows and arrows laid idle in their quiver. In history, whenever any attempt for molestation or rape of a tribal women made by any outsider be it Indian or British the Andaman belligerents never spared the guilty. On 4th March 1858 two Britishers namely John P. Streeten and Maddock were killed by the natives when they attempted to molest a Great Andamanese woman at North Bay. On 28th June 1863 Naval Brigadesman Mr. Pratt was killed by two Great Andamanese after he tried to rape a Great Andamanese woman namely Hina alias Topsy during his earlier visit few months ago in January. The Andamanese members who killed Mr. Pratt the Britishers identified as Jumbo, her husband and TURA (another name Snowball?). But on 16 August 2002 when a Jarawa lady namely Lapa in hospital premises and a Great Andamanese girl namely Eleach D/o Smti Noe on 08 Octobar 2003 underwent rape attempts at Port Blair, the tribesmen were calm on the issue. There was no Jumbo or Tura. The accused in the case of molstation of LAPA was released on 17th August on bail within 24 hours of his arrest. He was charged with 'molestation' under section 354 of the Indian Penal Code, which happens to be a bailable offence. Molestation of the Jarawa girls at Tirur have become headlines in newspapers on countless days. There are many instances recorded recently which indicates a suspected but changing behaviour of the Jarawas. The women have also started permitting the outsiders to stay with them in their own camps. A group of

Jarawa girls themselves went to the JPP camps and mingled with the JPP staffs at Tirur. These girls paid visit to the villagers' farms and their houses. They worked for food in settlers' houses. On our enquiries they stood mute. That was a manifestation of the changing behavioural pattern of the tribal women — outcome of a constant monitoring by the villagers – not any anthropologist. In some cases sensitive in nature the close relationship of the Jarawa women with the outsiders raised the eyebrows of the authority such as (1) they stayed in farms of Muthu, a collinpur resident, (2)permitted Haren Mazumdar and his group to stay with them in Jarawa camp and the villagers offered them liquor, (3) allowed Theiry Falise a Bangkok based photojournalist to stay with them and take their attractive photographs, and (4) had friendly contact with Le-Figaro team from Paris in 2000 to the extent that reportedly they had sex with the Jarawa women. These innocent and honest tribes now as result of continued interaction with the outsiders are gradually becoming free of the values for which they are still respected by the intellectual ones. They demand money, pan, rice, tobacco, dal, and clothes and for sake of these items get ready to do anything for the donors. On enquiry by the officials in the matter they stand mute as promised to the donors. The saddest chapter is that instead of the fact that none can overpower a Jarawa woman, the Jarawa women would respond to sexual overtures of outsiders just for sake of some eatables. They are vulnerable to AIDS.

It is rightly said that the Jarawas are unpredicted. Though they are gradually cooling tribes and they come close to the poachers on just showing of a single pan or tobacco pouch, if physically threatened then never sit calm. In an incident, a Jarawa named Hoteile was killed at Mahua Tekri near Kadamtala by a group of fishers (and hunters?). On the day of the grave incident few fishermen intruded into the Jarawa territory on west coast and camped at one place near a Jarawa camp. A group of Jarawa came and asked for food when they were cooking. In the meantime as the Jarawas reported that the fishermen threw boiled water on one of the Jarawas. A fight was ensued between them in which Hoteile and a fisherman were killed. Non-bailable deterrent punishments may only keep the poachers away from the Jarawa and the Jarawa territory but due to lack of proper evidences/ witnesses and the Jarawas' incapability of express correctly in Hindi or English language the offenders always go free. Whether the role of Jarawa language translator in such cases be entertained should be discussed in decisive meetings.

The Jarawas are in general very simple people with simple thoughts. There is no difference between a poacher and a welfare activist for the Jarawas. Whoever gives anything to them they fit themselves into the donor's gamble. For this reason they invited outsiders as well as the welfare activists into their chada (hut) even in the night. But I must mention from my own experience that the Jarawas particularly the women have special feeling of affection for the functionaries of AAJVS which is little different from their views about the outsiders. The reason is that whenever they become sick or have health problem the AAJVS staff without delay take them to the nearest Primary Health Centre for treatment by vehicle and after recovery leave them safely at their habitat. On day basis the bananas were given to them from time to time now discontinued to promote their self- dependency. For the said reasons they developed a sense of affection and discipline towards the AAJVS staffs. It was an evening of May 2002, when I was on duty on ATR outside one community hut called 'Tulichada'. In the proximity, the road was blocked due to uprooting of a huge tree and the vehicles in a long convoy were stopped. The passengers were moving here and there in anxiety. For the next 2-3 hours it was not possible for the road to be free of the trunk as predicted looking to the size of the tree. Few of the passengers were lazily walking on the black road as if they were sleepwalking. The passengers were gradually scattered to different directions to pass the time by just roaming here and there. At that juncture my entire concentration was to observe the movement of the passengers and avoid their mingling with the Jarawas in the dark. After a while the light of the half moon was enough for us to see around. The forest workers in two or three on shift basis were engaged in chopping the huge trunk with help of their single hand saw. After few minutes we felt few rain drops on us. At the moment few Jarawa men and women with their flaring resin torches in hands came down from their hut to see what was going on. When I briefed the matter to them few women started pulling me and few pushing me to one direction to their hut while their husbands were standing near to them as if they told their wives to do so. The women requested in their language saying – Mappe nee ekade umoho (brother you sleep in our hut). What would be then, if any poacher is treated like this as they welcomed me? But as a protector of the rules it was not possible for me to break the same rules and accept their hearty welcome. The road got cleared at around 2000 Hrs. This was a simple and honest human expression from them. These teachers of humanity are able to teach us some lessons of life in such an easy manner that we may never find in our classroom. Are they the people who are presumed as the people of backward civilization and called to be junglee (referring to them in indecency in local parlance) or so by our so-called civilized society members? It is not so easy to shed an image that has been built over years that they were noxious for outsiders for their killing of outside people. Out of my numerous trips on duty to the Jarawa camps one such trip to the west coast I must mention about. It was a bright sunny day when our country boat touched the edges of the sand on west coast. Few Jarawa boys present there started somersaulting on hard surface of the wet sand while two of them threw themselves into the water in joy and began to demonstrate their diving skills. After a while three adult Jarawas who actually belonged to Tirur band Gena, Emohonda and Lewa appeared from the thicket. They carried my bag to give rest to my shoulders. The children after finishing their demonstrational play rushed to me. At the moment our Pharmacist found that one boy received a deep cut edged by a seashell on his right leg. He immediately treated and covered the injury with help of bandage. The Jarawas in joy holding my bag and medicine box of the Pharmacist started walking to their hut situated in the interior on a hillock. They told only 'chada alema'(come home). While walking with them one thing I clearly understood from the Jarawas teachers that 'Follow his tracks, whether it is marshy, leech-infested terrain or a walk through knee-deep water, he knows through practice, where to place his foot'. We started following them as good disciples in the column. The men were simply walking in front while the children were loping on the sides. After few minutes of walking I got terribly tired. Now we were listening to the patter of raindrops on dry leaves. But soon the rain stopped. I sat near a buttress and asked from one of them about how long to go. He replied, 'noda nadem, chada ekade bootte'(Not far away, our hut is near). After drinking little water we started walking. It was totally a dense forest. The top canopies of long trees were allowing only scattered sun rays to come down. The dry leaves being pressed beneath our soles were producing creaking sounds which were enough to give a sensation. The forest dwellers were walking so fast that in the meantime we had to run to join them. The beauty and majesty of a rainforest are indescribable. It is impossible to capture in any format of video, to describe in words, or to explain to those who have never had the awe-inspiring experience of standing in the heart of a primary rainforest. Can we guess how important the JARAWA RESERVE is, considering these example facts that - A single pond in Brazil can sustain a greater variety of fish than is found in all of

Europe's rivers. A 25-acre plot of rainforest in Borneo may contain more than 700 species of trees - a number equal to the total tree diversity of North America. A single rainforest reserve in Peru is home to more species of birds than are found in the entire United States. One single tree in Peru of South America was found to harbour about 43 different species of ants - a total that approximates the entire number of ant species in the British Isles. The number of species of fish in the Amazon exceeds the number found in the entire Atlantic Ocean. As I had very little ready knowledge comparing to the natives about the flora and fauna of the reserve, I was excited to know about them from the Jarawas themselves. It really may be interesting to conduct a taxonomical study with help of the Jarawas..but... the 'but' is but. When I began to ask about the surrounding trees, the natives with great enthusiasm started showing the trees with explanation and clear expression that these are theirs. To our notice one boy ran to his left and showed me a tree. It was a Kadamb tree (Anthocephalus Kadamba). They explained, they use the wood of it in construction of 'Uhu'(honey container). The 'Uhu' is made of single piece of wood dug out from inside and well designed at outer surface. The design is created with pig blood mixed with fat of wild boar/monitor lizard and red clay paste. They make a special cover of bottom inside the 'Uhu' with Bee wax. During the tracking they explained about the flora and fauna they saw on sides. Finally I reached their hut. A group of men, women and children in their traditional adornments were present in the hut. They offered us the pork as feast. Though we were hungry, we had to humbly refuse the offer. On our refusal to pork they offered to us some Khattaphal (Baccaurea sapida), a wild fruit called by them 'Keene'. The aborigines in the hut behaved with us in so caring manner as if their band members came back to them after a long exile. Thus, the breeze of hatred has no place in their cold valley of harmony. Our first Prime Minister Pt. Jawahar Lal Nehru once said, "Peace is not a relationship of nations. It is a condition of mind brought about by a serenity of soul. Peace is not merely the absence of war. It is also a state of mind. Lasting peace can come only to peaceful people". The way of their welcoming is incredible, admirable and heart touching. Much has been said almost critically about their observed outside behaviour, while very few know about the inner aspects of their behavioural pattern. Their simple begging and nudity can never be construed as their demand for food and cloth or they lack these things. When our children beg for chocolate or biscuit or pick up the same from the tea tray before a guest in the drawing room, we simply take this as a childish behaviour then why such simple behaviour of the Jarawas are taken in other sense? When our children go out to the street or to some distance we immediately run behind them in fear of any mishap, we simply never say that they went in hunger. Secondly, When they are on road, at the very same time if you pay a visit to their hut you will definitely find plenty of wild roots, tubers, fruits and pork hanging from the roof. As result of outside contact they have developed a sense to collect the salty eatables, sweets, chocolates, biscuits and bananas thrown out by the passengers. Who said that they don't have the sense of storing food and other items or have lack of policy for preservation? Yes! They keep thought for the future. A Health centre can be used as a ground for such observations. When a Jarawa is admitted for treatment, he from the date of admission starts preserving bread, biscuit, clothes and whatever he gets from the staffs and others in a bundle of bed sheet to take home. One day I found fungal infections in the bread (Natah) hidden in their parcels and then I had to persuade the Jarawa to throw the bread out, who finally in sad mood threw out his Natah packets. The Jarawas have a developed sense to preserve their forest resources for generations. For making chest guard they measure the requirement of the bark and peel off the bark from a tree of the same measurement which allows the tree for a quick recovery. Similarly they get edible roots and tubers from the matured plants. When they kill one pig, then don't run behind the another.

Obviously apart from the roads and village points, the hospitals and PHCs have become suitable places to study the changed and changing behaviour of the Jarawas. In the recent years the members who came as attendants with patients to the PHCs and hospitals remarkably increased in number. They were registered as 'Diet Patients'. Be it patient or attendant, all the Jarawas are tempted to camp at PHC or hospital for want of clothes, sleepers, food and fun with the outsiders. In a Jarawa hut when one member is supposed to be evacuated to the nearest PHC, the other member lay down near a hearth and deliberately heat the body. After a while when body becomes heat he pretends to be sick and says 'Me Ullede' means 'I am sick'. Such drama is played only to reach the health centre. Once in handling such a case our pharmacist was with me on the spot. When he tried to give few Paracetamol tablets he refused and became adamant to be evacuated to the health centre. On many occasions lactating mothers (mostly I observed Minodili a Jarawa lady of Tirur) also show their normal looking infants seeking hospital treatment of the baby. Despite we have attempted to reduce the number of fake patients and family attendants in their evacuations, the diet patients comparing to the actual patients increased because of our suspicion about the health problem and the unavoidable tribal sentiments. Sometimes these diet patients after spending few happy days in the medical ward demand for 'return to homes'. This is only a small component of our incomplete study of the Jarawas' changing behavior. If one child is evacuated then all the family members join the patient preferably the mother, father and small children.

8

Food

The Jarawas are moving in their territory in different bands mainly in search of food and water. Indigenously there is no concept of lunch, dinner and breakfast among the Jarawas. They collect most of their food items from their own territory, either from forest or from aquatic sources. Claws and skins of monitor lizards, shells of bivalves and gastropods, fish skeletons, carapace and chelipedes of crabs can be seen in their camping sites. There is no dearth of food in their territory. The aborigines practice boiling, roasting and baking. Sometimes I saw they prepared one food item in different ways to be consumable. Nowadays the Jarawas have started eating some food items, which they never consumed earlier. Prior to the recent contacts, a few non-traditional food items like banana and puffed rice were given to them as gifts by administrative contact teams. Now as a result of frequent noticed and unnoticed contacts with the outsiders they started to consume zarda pan, tobacco, alcohol(?), south Indian dishes available in shops and small hotels such as Idli, Dosa, Mitha appu, Murku, sweets, biscuits, chocolates, other snack items, rice, dal, spiced vegetables, and many other items. These food articles are procured by the Jarawas from the villagers, tourists, tour operators and vehicles, shopkeepers of the shops located at the jetties and from the policemen picketing near their *chaddas*. Thus they have developed a trend leading to ways to collect the salty eatables, sweets, chocolates, biscuits and bananas etc from the outsiders and got lingering tastes on their tongues. On an occasion one traveller urgued, "Giving food items (snacks) to them is not an offence, then why do you stop us in doing so? " Then I had to reply in brief how strange food items can cause genetic mutation and loss of immunity to the diseases commonly existing in our society but yet strange to them. It was my prime duty to explain but he had no time in hurriness of his journey to listen carefully.

The practice of procuring non-traditional food influences their foraging behaviour when they camp at or visit roads, jetties and villages. It has been found that when the Jarawas camp near the Andaman Trunk Road, the children and young members invariably spend much time of the day on the road. Though it is generally out of curiosity and to derive some entertainment, in the process they procure some food also. In fact some young boys stop all kinds of foraging activities except tourist hunting, as long as they camp close to the ATR. I observed this mostly when the Jarawas camped at R.K. Nallah, Putatang and Punanallah near the ATR. But the same group of people, while camping at places away from the road, do not simply bother about non-traditional items of food. They remove all their clothes when they stay near sea or in a hunting expedition to avoid brushing of clothes with thorns and bushes while chasing an animal.

In their indigenous dietary menu pig (*Sus scrofa andamanensis*) called 'Wowe' in their language is one of their prime food resources. On a hunt they first trace animal footprints, then they find the animal and kill it. On many occasions I made attempts to accompany them in their hunting expeditions in the dense but failed to run as they ran and finally I had to come back. Very occasionally I found that they took help of dogs like local poachers to hunt pig. After killing of a pig by arrows the visceral mass is removed by cutting ventral side of the abdomen by Towa, their cutting implement. The void space inside the body is then packed with licuala peltata leaves called 'Silaipatti' in local parlance. The hunter and companions customarily carry the prey to the hut. When it is ready to put on fire they remove the leaves out. The toes are detached from the body and the pig is made to sit on fire and after a while it is rolled on fire. The Jarawas of other areas usually come and join them in eating pork. Firstly the pig is burnt for removing the hairs and roasted for about half an hour. The pig is then beheaded. After that the pig is cut into several pieces and boiled for consumption. After eating pork they use a tooth pick called 'Mahu' by them. There is a difference in the preparation of pork between the Jarawas and the local settlers. The Jarawas initially burn the pig and remove very roughly the hairs form the skin with help of their traditional knife called 'Towa'and as result the lower layer of the skin contains plenty of pig hairs partially while the settlers at first soak the skin otherwise cover the skin with mud before burning and after burning scratch the skin with help of dao or knife in such a way that the hairs come out from their roots. The meat of pig is distributed among the members as per a particular custom. The man who shot the pig will get a particular portion of the pig while those who carried the prey in the way will get another special portion under their custom. On many occasions I observed that the hunter got the back portion of the pig. The boiled pork is usually hanged over the hearth or placed on a platform covered by Licuala leaves (*Licuala peltata*) over the fire. They do not touch the share of others even if they are hungry. In a usual hunting expedition wild boar becomes their major target followed by monitor lizard (*Varanus salvator andamanensis*) and turtle, apart from fishing. The meats of wild boar and monitor lizard contain good sources of energy. The processes of the hunting games are more or less uniform and very systematic; the individual variation is almost negligible. The Jarawas have traditionally no hunting method other than bow and arrow hunting. Now a days as result of learning from the local poachers they pitch hunting trap to catch wild boar. There is one observable variation due to seasonality in hunting of wild boar. In peak dry season (April- May) they try to avoid hunting the wild boar due to less amount of fat content. During this season they engage themselves in collection of honey and jackfruit. The settlers exploit considerable amount of forest resources, particularly the wild boar, which is the most essential energy resource for the Jarawas, apart from the marine resources. Hunting with less efficient tools like bow and arrow, the Jarawas are inefficients comparing to the commercial hunters, but they are still efficient enough for their subsistence through hunting. They procure their food from sea and forests under their subsistence economy which is directly and indirectly associated with their socio-cultural and ecological values too. After eating pork the Jarawa members decorate their faces, chests, hands, and stomach with mud. The women apply mud on their body parts including the abdomen. While applying on body they suck little mud. They do the same after honey consumption but interestingly the designs on their body parts become different for this time to signify that whether he or she has eaten pork or honey. They do believe that if they do this they will get more honey or pig in coming days joined by another belief that they keep the malevolent spirits away by doing this.

The skulls of turtles and wild boars can be seen hanged in different nets in a Jarawa Hut as marks of who hunted how many number of pig or turtle. In addition to the wild boar they consume monitor lizard, crab, fishes except few fishes like eel fish, turtle, turtle eggs, eggs of monitor lizard, edible shells like trochus (*Trochusnilo ficus*), bivalves, turbo (*Turbo maramaratus*) and rock oyster (*Saccostrea cucullata*), honey, crustaceans, larvae of honey bee, borer

(Cerambycidae) and other insects, etc as animal based diets. It may be noteworthy that the Jarawas in their traditional diet have no intake of leafy vegetables. The women do not consume monitor lizard for obscure reason. There are divisions of labour among them. Adult men mainly go to hunt pig and to fish and do other hard works while the women have the job of collection of fruits, roots, tubers, edible shells and crab hunting and fishing in shallow water. The women collect grubs of wood inhabiting beetles. They collect grubs from soil just underneath rotting logs. They consume flesh from inside the body of a crab and its chellate legs while very occasionally I saw them chewing tiny prawns in raw. Usually they boil prawns and lobster and remove their exoskeletons before consumption. When you are in a Jarawa territory you may probably see spotted deer (*Axix axis*), barking deer (*Muntiacus muntjac*) and number of birds like Parakeets, Doves, Kingfishers, Crow pheasants, Swifts, Bulbul, Andaman teal, and White breasted water hen, etc. But I wish you not to meet some venomous snakes like Branded krait, Pit vipers, Kobra and a centipede (*Scolopendra subspinipes debaani*) commonly known as 'Kankhajura' which is quite notorious for its painful bite.

It is important to note that they do not consume deer and most of the birds (Noha) as spiritual taboo. Spotted deer and barking deer (*Muntiacus muntjac*), two common animals are found in the Jarawa Reserve forests, but the Jarawas do not hunt them for food. The barking deers being shy in nature are mostly found in the dense forests of the Baratang, Middle and North Andamans. It has been named after its call, which bears a striking resemblance to the bark of a dog. They rarely venture out into open lands and sometimes seen near the edge of the road. In the Jarawa Reserve the wild pig and spotted deer are two common choices of the poachers. But these days they (Jarawas) hunt them for others. Despite they don't eat most of the birds they target them with pointed arrows to enhance the shooting skill. Now many Jarawa boys can be seen using 'Gulel' learnt from the ranchi labourers to hit the birds. The Gulel traditionally used by the ranchi people of forest villages is made of two small wood pieces crossed and tied with help of a strip of rubber or piece of rubber tube of a tyre. The 'V' gap of the 'Y' or 'X' shaped 'Gulel' is used to aim the target, and rounded stones are shot with help of the rubber strip. Apart from it, I saw many Jarawa children cruelly playing with swiflet birds roped from their legs but they never tried to consume them. For reasons, snake (tompo), rat (miye), few kinds of bird (noha), frog (ethe), etc. are not included in the Jarawa Dietary Menu. They do not kill crocodile (heirugya) for food because they believe that the crocs are homes to some benevolent spirits.

They use a strange fruit as food only after a bird is seen eating it. The fruits mostly are consumed right after the collection in the forest. Let me mention in their own words what kinds of fruit and seeds they consume. They consume Aab (wild Jackfruit), Keen (*Baccaurea ramiflora* or locally called Khattaphal), Otang (*Calamus andamanicus* Kurz), Gee (*Rubus moluccanus*), Jiggi (*Diascorea glabra*), bagatho, Umin(Cycas rumphii), Omenad, Lectang (*Donax cannaeformis*), Konothoa, Chone (wild banana), Daug (*Cocos nucifera* L.), Yeha, Impo, Leidan, Wakam, Lokei, Thuya, Torka and many others not identified. One more fruit locally called Khadi khajur (*Phoenix paludosa*) they consume as I observed. One day I was given by them a piece of wild mango (*Mangifera andamanica*) called 'Aphey' by them. The Jarawa female members use some fruits as their ornaments. The yellow Khattaphal fruits when available in plenty are used as necklace, garland, waist girdles, and head band. It is interesting to see that when any fruit is collected by women abundantly they on the spot adorn themselves with those fruits to carry the same and bring home. They slice into pieces the Umin, keep in net collected from shore and dip the same into sea water for some time. After that they hang the same net from the roof of hut and just before consumption boil in fresh water. As result of their administrative contacts the banana (not wild banana) became gift food for them. They consume riped bananas while green bananas are consumed only after boling or roasting. The Jarawas eat many kinds of seed, some are eaten raw and some are boiled or roasted. The seeds of 'Aab' (wild jackfruit) and 'Uiyaw' have very important place in the Jarawa dietary menu in the category of edible seeds. I noticed that in addition to the animal based food there are more than 50 items in the traditional diet menu of the Jarawa in the category of "fruit, nut, seed, root and tuber". The women when camped near the ATR, come onto the road and dig earth along the road side with help of iron sticks to collect a wild tuber called 'Jyev' by them. They sing a very special Jyev song while collecting Jyev. Sometimes while collecting 'Jyev' I saw few women chewing junglee pan (Piper betel) to which they referred as 'Intoto'. The settlers in past used to enter the reserve from Shoal Bay area for collection of pan to sale in the domestic market. These days it may be observed that there is an increase in the consumption of pan among the aborigines. They began to consume tobacco leaves (narcotics) locally called 'Suckha' as acquired habit. In the deep forest when they don't find water then there is no problem for them. They immediately cut and divide the stem of Calamus andamanicus kurz (arecaceae) and drink the juice oozing out from the stem called 'Ottang' by them.

In process of the honey collection a Jarawa man ties with the body some leaves of a plant called 'Uya' to drive the bees (Onyoma).After consuming honey called 'Lev' he usually goes to bath because as calorific value of honey is very high it enhances the body heat. Their bathing at this time has another reason. The stickiness of honey on body causes uneasiness unless washed off through bathing. Importantly I noticed that they never threw the bee wax into fire. The

Jarawas collect honey of two types of honey bees viz. *Apis dorsata* and *Apis cerana indica*. Before the start of April, the month of joy and happiness the Jarawas start making honey container called 'Uhu' by them. An 'Uhu' is preferably made of Kadamb tree (Anthocephalus) but block of other trees are also used. The wooden block is scooped from inside and given the shape of a bucket without handle. The handle is made of tree barks. The bottom of 'Uhu'from inside is covered by Bee wax. The size of 'Uhu' may vary from ten litres capacity to fifty litres capacity. One day while walking with the Jarawas in the forest I saw a man made pit in earth in a large area appearing to have something in the earth. On asking from the Jarawas they unearthed the area and finally I saw there was a large Uhu of around 200 Litres capacity made from a single and large tree trunk. The Uhu was containing honey upto the neck and after that it was covered with licuala leaves thickly and then the pit was closed. The Jarawas explained that they had stored the honey here for consumption in near future. During an enquiry into a case of a Jarawa raid, the Jarawas helped us see Uhu of the same size (about 200 litres capacity) sealed with full of honey and buried near a Jarawa camp at Dhaninallah. Unfortunately the poachers had destroyed the honey stored for the future. Looking to the destroyed honey the Jarawas made serial raids into the adjacent forest villages.

9

The Material Culture

In the Jarawa community small children are routinely allowed to play with sharp knives (Towa), Dao (a cutting implement) and burning objects without adults paying any attention to them. The adult members say that this will help them (children) learn many things without their guidance.

The Jarawas' aesthetic culture reflecting from their baskets, tools, implements, weapons and other containers are enough to enchant art lovers and connoisseurs alike but as result of the continuous contact with the outsiders their material culture has also come into the transition and the old art is being permanently avoided. In addition to their cane, bamboo and wooden baskets they started to use plastic and aluminum containers and cooking vessels. We in our line of duty on many occasions (for example- March-April 2006) distributed among them aluminum degchi (called 'Busu' by them) to boil meat, Dao, a cutting implement commonly used by the local settlers, Chisel, Triangular file, spade, axe, hammer, and iron plate, etc. with the administrative purpose to encourage their hunting, fishing and gathering activities and prevent them from intrusion into the adjacent villages for want of these items. The great change is observed communally in their material culture especially in their food and clothing. Now one can easily find in their any camp, the non-traditional items such as Match box(Tuh), readymade garments, polythene sheet, plastic jerrycan, gunny bags, sickle, chisel (Togitah), File (Thotache), Iron Plate (Tah or Tahotopia), hammer (Chodaveda), axe(Thotal), Adze (Pelaita), Dao(Thotikeli), HandSaw (Thondav), shinestone, Knife, Blade, shoe, sleepers, plastic bottles, metal bowl, belt, mirror, metal chain, wool bundle, soap, bangle, tobacco, pan, zarda, brush, sunglass, cap, hanky, and hair oil etc.

Significantly, many ready things which are routinely used by the Jarawas never became parts of their mainstream material culture. For example: Sleepers and various kinds of containers made of rubber and plastics are often brought on shores by the waves since their inventions but the Jarawas ofcourse used them but never used them in the way to be purely dependants on them. It may be understood that they do not like to have footwear which may obstruct them in their hunting and fishing games. Similarly they continued their hard and long works in making baskets and buckets with help of wood, canes and bamboos instead of collecting the alternative items from the shores. Actually they love to weave their own baskets of various patterns and designs and they as cultural hobby decorate their wooden buckets such as 'Uhu' to be handed over with the native art from one generation to another.

The present Jarawas have many introduced materials and methods such as pitching of hunting trap, wearing of clothes and sleepers, washing of clothes with soaps, use of powder and hair oil, etc. But as a matter of satisfaction the melting pot of their culture has still some indigenous values in forms of simple tools, implements, huts, containers and ornaments. They do all works of art with help of the materials available in their own territory. Their eco friendly material culture is deeply associated with other aspects of life. Their bows and arrows are often used in hunting and fishing activities but if required they may use them against the poachers. The men make their hunting implements such as bows (called by them 'Aao'), arrows (called by them 'Patho') and chest guard (called by them 'Tohe'). For making iron heads of arrows and the traditional knife 'Towa' they collect metal pieces from wrecked ships and adjacent villages. I have never seen any female member using bow, arrow and chest guard. Their material culture is strongly associated with their gender values. When small children target any bird in play with toy bows and toy arrows, among them the girls do not do this. For making bow mainly the wood of chooi (Sagerea elliptica) is used. For collecting chooi wood called 'Totanpa' by them, sometimes they enter the forests in the Baratang island. I noticed this when I was deputed at Middle Strait and I had to record the daily movement of the Jarawas with purposes in prescribed column of Jarawa Movement Register. The bowstring called 'Betho' is made from fibres of climbers known as 'Waye' and 'Weibo' and sometimes they use bark strip of a particular tree (Anodendron manubrium). The size of a bow is depending on the hunter's choice and his ability to use. Big bows are generally used by adult healthy men. Their iron adze tied with wooden handle is called 'toub'. The Jarawas construct different kinds of arrows (Patho) for different purposes. Their wooden head arow is made of Arecca Wood (*Arecca trianda*). One type of arrow stick is called 'Ochokia 'by them. They use iron and areca wood or Bamboo to make iron head arrow called 'aetaho' in their language. One more Iron head arrow is constructed by them which is called 'ochchale tahape' in the native language and they use iron and chuiwood to construct it. Their harpoon arrow is called 'tahowai khoab' which is constructed with the use of iron, cane and areca wood. During my camping in a Jarawa hut of Punnanallah area I observed mainly two types of weapon viz. 'Thom' and 'Thosulatetoha'. 'Thom' is a Jarawa word called for pointed iron arrow, the head of which generally is found with the length of 4-5 inches. Thosulatetoha is an iron arrow head while its supporting stick is called 'thena' by the Jarawa. Mainly the stem of *Oxytenanthera nigrociliata monro* is used in making of 'Thena'. The metal head is sharpened on a piece of stone called 'Ulli'. It may also be interesting to observe that they put into fire very rarely the metal head of arrow to give shape. They in general do not use the technique as our blacksmiths use in making iron tools and implements. Once a metal plate is collected they first get the size by cutting it with help of chisel. Earlier only iron piece or track piece of log trains were used as hammer in cutting, edging and giving shapes to the metal item. Now, some Jarawas adopt heat and hammer technique in making of sharp iron head like a modern blacksmith. But generally they still use the primitive techniques in which they only beat the plate from the start to completion with hammer or an iron piece using as hammer to make leaf shaped arrow heads. Once the arrow head is ready it is fixed to a bamboo shaft (Thenang) and tied with the string which is made of a climber (Weibo). There after the tied portion (Topijae) is waxed. The women were never seen fishing with help of bows and arrows. Yes, they used small fishing harpoons to pierce and pull the tiny fishes from their rock holes. They collect nylone nets from the sea shore to make their small net bag to store their collected stuffs and mainly fish. They also construct their fishing handnet with bark, bamboo and cane and call it 'potochehut'. They generally use fishing nets (called by them as 'Botho') to fish in shallow water. Now a days interestingly a unique kind of arrow I have seen, they are using. They fix small iron bolts on head of bamboo or wooden stick to shoot birds which is called 'Nohathini' or 'Nohathena'. While dealing with the Jarawas I always stayed away to the possible extent from the persons who carried 'Towa' with them. This was not because of fear of their attack but a manual accident. 'Towa' is the most popular and common implement among the Jarawas. Apart from the Towa their indigenous knife made of stone is called 'ulihe'. The Towa has a shape of an arrow with no stick but has a wide breadth of 4-6 inches. They keep Towa in their chest guard called 'Tohe/Kekad' in Jarawa Language. The Towa is made of metal plate traditionally keeping both the edges sharped in order to use this cutting implement from both the sides. They use Towa mostly to cut meat, beehives and plant fibers. The special feature of the Towa is that it has no handle and the Jarawas hold it from its flattened end with both the sharp edges tightly gripped by their bare hands. As a change they started using Towa in another way. They use it to threat the outsiders by waving it in front of them. In doing so the outsiders cannot capture the Towa because of its fast waving and one end in length which is flattened is gripped by the native and the other end of the towa has so sharp conical shape that even a touch of it can cut your finger. The flattened end of the knife is rapped thinly with the string of Tha-an, an orchid (Dendrobium). Normally a Jarawa places his knife and other flat tools between the layers of his chest guard (called 'Tohe' or sometimes 'Kekad' by them) made of bark of a tree (Stracula vilosa). The chest guard is used by the adult male members during hunting and gathering activities in forest. In their previous battles against the other ethnic groups the chest guard worked as Arrow proof jacket. They keep two layers of bark strip in a chest guard. Both the ends of the bark strips are neatly stitched together with threads extracted from the same bark. Now plastic thread is also used in the stitching work. A very unique thing I observed that when a member has to construct a chest guard he initially takes measurement of his chest and cuts only the limited portion of the bark he requires to make his chest guard. In our so- called civilized world we are not so much ecologically cautious as they are. Their digging stick of iron is called 'wohen'. Before the beginning of April they must complete 'Uhu' their honey container. From January- February onwards all the men and women engage themselves in making of honey container.

The 'Uhu' is traditional wooden bucket generally used in collection and storage of honey. The block of Anthocephalus kadamba wood (Thadda) is scooped from inside and given the shape of a bucket without handle. The Uhu of taung peing wood is also used by them. The handle is made of tree barks. The bottom of 'Uhu' from inside is covered by Bee wax. The out portion is decorated with attractive zig- zag designs with help of pig blood and fat of pig/monitor lizard and /or red clay paste. The women show a unique sense of colour combination in their art of basketry. When a Jarawa woman makes cane basket (Taj) she sings the songs which revolve around her collection of Jyev(wild tuber), fruits, larvae, crabs and tiny fishes. The high degree of concentration is reflected from their works. To build a good combination of colours with strong weaving they use plastic threads of different colours collected from the sea shore. It is exciting and heart winning to see in a Jarawa basket from bottom to top the art of colouring e.g. red above blue and above that yellow and above that green and again red and above that not blue this time but any other colour contradictory to red. Thus with availability of plastic threads of only few limited colours the women make their cane and bamboo baskets so much attractive and technically correst that we must accept that they themselves are the authority. The young girls of the Jarawa community learn the tribal art to carry and preserve for the future. Their unique talent as a carver is not a single result of any formal study or training, but has been completely self taught and evolved from their heartfelt inspiration. The women in order to construct attractive cane baskets vertically place pencil canes only while horizontally the basket is layered by plastic thread of various colours. On some occasions I found baskets made of only canes and/or bamboo without using plastic thread. They construct their baskets in accordance with their future use. The male members never do this work. The strip of Calamus Palustris is also used in making of basket.

How fire (Tuh) came into them is still a mystery unsolved. Since the time immemorial they keep burning and carry fire from one camp to another. They use their traditional resin torch called 'Tuh- phone' or 'Tuh - ga' while moving in night. Now in this context they became worriless after the introduction of match boxes. Traditionally they make their torch with help of *Licuala peltata* leaves/ spinosa which are together rolled and then filled with resin collected from the tree of *Parishia insignis* and *Caneriam euphyllum*. They are still using their own resin torches because match stick of few inches cannot burn for hours. They hang the match boxes over their hearths to keep it warm perhaps learnt from the local villagers. Sometimes the Jarawas use thin plastic ropes and threads removed from the fishing nets found on shore in making of bows, arrows, baskets, buckets, torches and chest guards, etc. But generally they use bark strips, plant fibres and stem ropes (Inetoe) to bind, tie and weave or stitch in their material works. The thick bark strip of *Hibiscus tiliaceus* is used by the women for carrying babies in their movements. Similarly they use bark strip to tie metal head with its wooden handle to finally make a small spade which is generally used in Uhu making. As a result of learning from the local poachers the Jarawa boys sometimes do not carry bows and arrows with them in hunting. They carry twigs and plastic ropes to pitch hunting traps in the forest. They have learnt from the local poachers and the APWD workers working on the ATR about the method to pitch trap to hunt animals. Surprisingly on many occasions I noticed that they used damaged accelerator wires of motorcycles and scooters instead of plastic ropes in pitching of hunting traps. Those wires were removed and brought from the other traps pitched by the local poachers in their reserve. I always tried to suggest the Jarawas not to use the techniques of trapping the animals. Usually the traps are pitched at more than 5-6 spots and sometimes 10-15 spots and after pitching they go unchecked at time. In such conditions the trapped animals die and decomposed before the advent of hunter. Thus the number of animals killed is more than the number of animals being consumed. Secondly the trapping techniques can make the Jarawas lazy and fortune hunters further leading to the loss of confidence in their own skill of hunting. But in the mainstream Jarawa society, the adult members make toy bows and toy arrows for their children. The making of containers, bows, arrows, resin torch, and some adornments of varied sizes and designs are some major observable artforms, which they carried with them since very begining. In their material culture, the present Jarawas do not know the art of making canoe. Sometimes they used simple water rafts made of bamboo and logs to cross the creeks and channels. In 1790 Colebrook closely saw few tribes plying a canoe near the present Dandaspoint of South Andaman. Some of their words collected by him were found to be of the Jarawa language. Yet another report informed that the Jarawa had canoes. "On 16th November,1884 Portman's expedition enchored near the Cinque Island when they saw some smoke coming out of the jungle. Three canoes of the Jarawas found there, were kept on board. Oldham, the incharge of operation captured and brought nine of them to Port Blair and after a long stay they were taken back and made free." These reports lead us to assess that the Jarawas had canoes about 220 years ago. But those canoes were collected from the shore or won as a War -Trophy in their battles against neighbouring tribes or they themselves constructed the canoe, is not finally confirmed. But we must not forget the fact that the Jarawa and the Onge (Onges are skilled in canoe making) were one tribe at one time in past now territorially separated. If they knew the art of canoe making then when and how the Jarawas gave up the construction of canoe? or how did they forget the art of making canoe? or is it correct that both the tribes (Onge and Jarawa) once never had canoe and after a long period only the Onges learnt to make canoe? constitutes an important topic for our further research. Similarly the

Onges in early period knew the art of pottery and few senior Onges I interacted still do know the art but practically do not do this and the Jarawas had no knowledge about the pottery.

The observations revealed that the Jarawas have fast learning capacities. The Jarawas of Middle Andaman sometimes manufacture roughly but usable wax candles with help of wax of the behives, a bamboo piece and cotton or wool as wick of candle. They learnt the art of making candle merely by watching the settlers' using candles in forest villages and in the Primary Health Centres. On the other hand, as the Shompens make fire generator, the Jarawas never developed any art or method to create fire or to make salt like that of the Dani tribe. The salt is newly introduced item while they have been using 'Fire' since the time immemorial. The Dani people of Papua (Irian Jaya) dive banana leaves into the sea water where they absorb the salty water. Later they burn the leaves and use the ash as salt. By giving this example I am not emphasizing on the art of salt making knowing that the Jarawas in their mainstream are still not using salt in their traditional diets. I exampled 'the Dani' only to express that few such techniques the Jarawa never developed. They (Jarawas) never invented any technique to block the traffic flow of the road despite the fact that they communally always hated the road users. Every tribal community and every member carry talents of the levels vary from one individual to another. It is believed that the Jarawas do not know the art of pottery while the Onges had 'Pottery' ('Wey' in Onge language) now extinct in their material culture. I have in my collection some rare pieces of earthern pots, discovered in 2007 from a kitchen midden of an abandoned community hut namely 'Tambebui Beyra' near the Onge settlement at Dugong Creek. The Onges are ancient foragers and it is still astonishing to hear about the pottery from some of their living members. But they are not able to answer on 'When?' and 'How?'. It is also to mention that the oldest piece of pottery was found in China and dates back to 7900 BC. Pottery was not only an early invention, but also one of our first art forms. Similarly the Jarawa never developed any musical instrument like 'Bomu' of Great Andamanese. The human talent, the outside contact, the ecology, the available resources, the socio-cultural norms, incidents, the contemporary circumstances and many other things, woven with each other, attribute to the development and/or changes in aspects of a tribal community. This is the reason behind why the Andaman tribes, groupwise differ from one to another in context of their art, culture and wisdom. These days, few Jarawas speak fluently good Hindi while their compatriots use few words only. Few boys easily would start my office bike by kicking and accelerating on neutral point during my patrolling in the Jarawa area while few of them just watched curiously my ride on the monster. The Jarawas are like other world tribes at the stage of 'initial contacts' which may compel them to learn or develop many things. Now with the 'initial contacts' they began to know about the use of salt and other things. Not withstanding the Dani, the Jarawas, instead of developing their own techniques to procure salt (as exampled) and other items, are gradually becoming fully dependants on salt packet, match box, and other items which further may lead them to voluntarily come close to the poachers for want of these things.

10

Dress and Ornaments

Interstingly, among the Jarawas there is complete absence of body incisional tattoos, fetishist scarification, ethnic piercings, lip plates like that of Mursi tribe of Ethiopia, the penis guard as used by Onge of Little Andaman, Dani and Yali tribes of Papua (Irian Jaya), Lip-plugs as used by the Eskimo of Alaska, earlobes (Shompen tribe), the traditional ritual body markings, tribal magic and religion like many other tribal communities of the world. The Jarawas of both sexes are generally mother naked. However some ornaments are worn by them and these are to express their cultural ethnicity. The adorning articles used by the Jarawa are head band, necklace, armlets and waist bands. These are mainly made of palm leaves, shells, bark, fruits and flowers. The Thuiya leaves (Dhani leaves) called "Popo' by them are generally used by the women to cover and adorn themselves. The women use tender leaves dissected from *Musa sapientum* (wild banana) as head band and from the headband artificial hairs made of the sharp strips of leaves come down together to cover the chest. Notably the Jarawa women never adorn themselves in pregnancy. Once during my camping at Badabalu (West coast) I noticed few Jarawa women adorned their necks and waists with help of sea weeds called 'Alẹi' by them while few women garlanded themselves with cowries (Cypraea caputserpentis). Few women used the money cowries (Cypraea moneta) as waist girdles. A frill of shells (especially cowrie) tied with a bark strip or rope called 'Lelele' is generally worn by a woman. The Jarawa women carry their children on their backs with the help of bark belts, weight of which is given on mother head. It is called 'keka' by them.

The Jarawa women have a great spirit to use flowers of attractive colours as ornaments. They love to sing and dance wearing floral ornaments in leisure period. Hokotat, Didoo, Inetua, Antang, Tulug, Aluk, Leedan, Impo, Uiyaw, Keen, Bada, Oha etc are native names of few of their ornaments made of flowers and fruits. Looking to the flowers of Gurjan tree (Dipterocarpus) on their bodies as ornaments one can easily guess that the honey collection season is yet to start. The edible ripped fruits of their ornaments such as Khattaphal (Baccaurea ramiflora) are eaten one after another and finally you may see nothing in the body. I was once surprised to observe that a woman was adorning herself with jungle supari (Areca triandra) called 'Thad' but she did not consume the nuts. I must mention here that the other present neighbouring tribes of Andamans like the Great Andamanese and the Onges are madly addicts to the wild arecanut.

As result of the frequent contacts with the outsiders, they started their journey from wearing scanty clothes to dirty pant- shirt with dirty and torn underwears. Once on my duty I found a boy namely Puhu standing near a jetty. It was irritating to me looking to his shirt fixed in his dirty pant with help of a damaged belt. The buttons of his gifted shirt was popped off. There was a red cap on his head. This is the usual costume of the present Jarawas when they are out of their abode forests. On many occasions they got used Khaki uniforms from the police staffs. Sometimes they do not simply wear one pant and shirt/ T shirt but wear double shirts with double pants with double underwears. These ill fitted clothes generally are full of dust and mud. The reason behind their getting such pattern of clothing is that when they are gifted a cloth item they without changing the cloth immediately wear over the clothes already he has on his body. Such types of clothing have caused several cases of fungal infections among them. Allergy could be the other result.They have obtained different types of readymade garments ('Kangapo') like bermuda, half pant, shirt, T-shirt, maxi, frocks and sleepers by the AAJVS when hospitalized. The synthetic clothes made of polyester, rayon, nylon, terelene or some other materials are not suitable to the Jarawas because of the following reasons. Firstly, the threads prepared out of the above mentioned materials are impermeable to water and they do not absorb sweat produced by the body during summer. Secondly, when sweat evaporates from the body surface it does not escape through these threads as they are thickly interwoven and a film of moisture always remains in between the clothes and the body.

The administrative parties during their contact expeditions gave them red clothes as gifts which the Jarawas used as their headbands. The Jarawas began to make their waist girdle and head bands with help of wool collected from the outsiders instead of leaves and fronds. The headband is called in Jarawa language 'aanotahe' while armlet is called 'Oetahe'. The name of their waist girdle is 'wayetahe'. Remarkably, they have some adornments when they become sick. The leaves of *Myristica andamanica* called 'Oro' by them is used when they become sick (Ullede). A kind of fronds is wrapped around the body to get relief from cough, cold and light fever. They use particular leaves stitched together to tie around the head against fever. Some leaves are used as coagulant against the leech-bite. In all such cases the leaves are systematically arranged with both the purposes i.e. to get cured from the disease and to adorn themselves.

On many occasions I found them adorned with small bones preferably mandible and clavicle of the lovable and respected members of their community after their deaths. Now the Jarawas have accepted to adorn themselves with metal and plastic chain, locket, bangels, and other kinds of duplicate jewels received from the outsiders.

11

Health and Hygiene

The Jarawas in tradition and ethnically have some health practices and knowledge of medicines. The Sub-Group of Experts recommended in 2006 that – In-situ treatment should be provided to the extent possible and use of traditional medicines of the Jarawa be encouraged. Alternate systems of medicine may also be introduced after due research. Further it was recommended that the ethno-medicine of the Jarawa needs to be documented. It may also be very interesting to note that almost all the botanical medicines are not used as oral intake. All the ethnobotanical medicines are externally applied on affected parts of the body. After eating pork they apply clay on mouth and other parts of the body to keep away the malevolent spirits and diseases. They cut their hairs regularly and take bath right after they consumed honey. Honey, one of their major foods is a great medicine for the Jarawas. Honey, a most assimilable carbohydrate compound, has distinct germicidal properties and in this respect greatly differs from milk which is an exceptional good breeding ground for bacteria. The universal and natural craving for sweets of some kind proves best that there is a true need for them in the human system. The Jarawa children who expend lots of energy have a real 'passion' for sweets. This is really instinct. Proteins will replace and build tissues but it is the function and assignment of carbohydrates to create and replace heat and energy, and to provide what we call honey, which contains two invert sugars, levulose and dextrose, has many advantages as a food substance. During my field work among the Jarawas one officer opined that their short stature is the result of poor nutrition. First of all, I am of the view that there is no scarcity of food in the Jarawa reserve. Secondly some of the world's tallest tribes such as Kenya's Maasai and Samburu typically suffer from poor nutrition. According to some experts human pygmies around the world are smaller than average because they tend to live very short lives which need more confirmations. But it is well known to all of us that stature is the result of an evolutionary process woven into Jarawa's genetic structure and would not change quickly. The short statured Negritos are found all over the world from Brazil to Papua New Guinea.

The female members of the community clean their genitals after urination and defecation by stick/twigs/leaves. The natives use sometimes a twig of *Pongamia pinnat* (Karanj) called 'Aichun' for cleaning teeth. A woman during her menstruation period and after parturition is made to sit on Licuala or palm leaves or stem of jungle supari (Thad) to keep control over the bleeding. As per my another observation, part of a special plant called 'Tidba' is used in menstruation to place near genitals or clean it. A type of climber called 'Kayatho' is used as bandage. During delivery of child umbilical cord is cut with help of their traditional knife 'Towa' and the placenta (Inepak) is covered and tied in leaf and then tied on a tree with some spiritual belief yet unknown. After the delivery the wild tuber called 'Jyev' is restricted for the mother for sometime. Most importantly the 'Umin' is not consumed by the women during pregnancy. It is believed by them that it causes birth of white babies in troublesome delivery if eaten. After the delivery the new born baby is massaged with fat of monitor lizard. The women lactate their babies for about 6-8 months but little water, small slices of pig fat and honey are also given to the babies. But honey is avoided in the first stage of lactation. The honey is also avoided by them during stomach pain. The natives have specific clay (Alame) treatment in case of fever, pain, cold and cut. The locally known Junglee Haldi called 'Paral' in Jarawa language and scientifically known as *'Curcoma zedoria'* is also used against fever and headache particularly among the infants. A herbal medicine is also used as preventive measure against snake bite. Stem pith of a plant called 'Endao' is used to stop vomiting and against the stomach pain.

In collection of the honey the stem of Jangli Haldi plant called 'Uya' is tied with the body and some parts chewed in mouth and the juice is thrown on the bee hives to drive away the honeybees (Onyoma). The booty leaves are given a heat and applied on body against cold, pain and fever. Though they are still away from the modern practices of health and hygiene, I noticed externally during my long work among them that rarely the Jarawa members carried dental ailments, cataract problems and throat problems. I have not seen any Jarawa with physical disability by birth. Since this is out of my clinical ability, I cannot mention absolutely in completeness about the diseases to which the Jarawas are still immune. But I strongly predict that with the intakes of alien food items their genetic mutation may definitely gear up resulting in communal damage of the small tribe. During my work period I on numerous occasions escorted the Jarawas between their habitations and hospital/health centre and I found their blood group to be either 'O' or 'A' mentioned in their clinical reports. In 1970s two Jarawa babies were found alive after a skirmish. They were found to be of group 'O'. Similarly, in 1930 five adult Jarawas were tested and they were found to be of group 'O'. The scientists still do not know exactly why there is an erratic distribution of bood group among the human groups and how they function in context of the resistance to diseases. We are still in search of the one answer about the genetic drift among the Andaman tribes and how their immune systems work. Our medical experts opine that the negrtio tribes are possible carriers of Sickle cell anaemia. Sickle cell anaemia is a disease in which our blood cells make'wrong' haemoglobin (the pigment of the red blood cells). The normal haemoglobin has a capacity to carry oxygen to various tissues. When one is afflicted by Sickle cell anaemia, this capacity is drastically reduced. The normal frequency of carriers of Sickle cell hamaeglobin genes is one several thousand in mosts parts of the world. However, in Africa, this frequency is 20 %. And if you carry Sickle cell haemoglobin gene, your red blood cells become impermeable to the malarial parasite and you thus become resistant to malaria. But in case of the present Jarawas a deep study is needed to reach a concluding end. However, on the other side of the coin, the Jarawas keep burning white dhup (Canrium euphyllum) and produce thick smoke inside their hut to drive out the mosquitoes but its efficacy is suspected on ground of the fact that a large number of the Jarawas were affected by the Malaria outbreak noticed in the year 2001. From February 2001 to January 2002, 90 cases of malaria (*Falciparum malaria* and *Plasmodium vivex malaria*) among the Jarawas treated in the PHC Kadamtala. From January to June in the year 2000, 37 cases of Mumps reproted from the Jarawa community of Kadamtala area. Remarkably, during that period the Jarawas patients used to come batch wise from different habitats of Middle and South Andaman. Before that in 1998 the Jarawa community acquired pneumonia and in September 1999 there was an outbreak of measles affecting nearly half of the Jarawa population. Surprisingly, in the year 1998 – 2002, total 1127 Jarawa cases have been treated in the PHC Kadamtala.The authority should not forget that the infectious diseases and serious epidemics were one of the main reasons for the decline in Andamanese numbers. Immediately after the contacts with the outsiders, diseases unknown to the Andamanese began to spread among them. The epidemics of pneumonia (1868), syphilis around 1876, ophthalmia (1876) and smallpox (1876), measles (1877), mumps (1886), influenza (1892) and gonorrhea (1892) dwindled the Andamanese population rapidly. In this regard the Sentinelese are perhaps the lucky people that they are not in our friendly contact or say 'Disease Contact'. The diseases like Respiratory Tract Infection (RTI), diarrhoea, skin diseases, hepatitis, fever, abdominal pain, indigestion, cold and cough are the common health problems existing among the Jarawas. At this juncture before we completely understand the 'JARAWA BIOLOGY' their forthwith vaccination against any disease may harm them to any extent and from any angle. Such kind of vaccination may cause gene mutation leading to loss of the strong immunity system which perhaps prevents them from many diseases known to us. There is no reporting of blood pressure, diabetics and many other diseases of serious nature among them. The Jarawas do not like to get injected needle, when hospitalized for treatment. During a field study by a medical team, a girl was fainted when niddle was inserted into her vein for taking her blood sample. The fellow native members aggressively started throwing of stones, sticks and arrows (by hands not through bows) towards the medical team members. Somehow the situation was brought under control with help of some senior Jarawas. But the Jarawas communally have accepted the modern modes of treatment because of their quick curing results. Meanwhile few pharmacists were appointed by the AAJVS who used to visit their huts and give medicines on the spot. Apart from this when a Jarawa patient is referred to nearest primary health centre he is accompanied by his family members and they all become ready to go to the PHC with the limited greediness to have some clothes, biscuits and chocolates as gifts from the outsiders during their stay at the PHC. After discharge of the Jarawas from a hospital, the prescriptions with medicines with verbal instructions about dosages are given to the official attendant who takes the discharged Jarawa back to their forest. Sometimes the attendants hand over the Jarawa patient, medicines and prescription to another staff of AAJVS, and forget to say about the dosages, verbally told to him by the pharmacist/nurse or doctor. In that situation the medicine course remains discontinued. The prescriptions are generally not systematically arranged by the AAJVS functionaries and if arranged then they cannot prepare an analytical record with help of them, because as I found, a doctor's prescription cannot be easily read even by the educated. The better the doctor, the worse is his handwriting. However, the doctors easily understand someone else's prescriptions due to their familiarity with the medical terms. Is the prescription meant for the patient or the doctor community? Prescriptions are written in great hurry. Generally 1-1 is written against shortcut name of medicine, to confuse whether dosage to be given two times After meal or Before meal? Instead it should be written 1A-1A(after meal) or 1B-1B(before meal). Can we make the communication a bit friendlier for the field functuionaries through simple steps so that they can give medicine to the Jarawa on time in appropriate dosage? The medical reports are like ancient scripts for an ordinary man. How does a field functionary attending a discharged Jarawa patient or even the best of literates understand their sickness from such a report so that they can deal with it? It is finally the AAJVS functionary who needs a precise understanding of the case to fight it rather than the doctor or pharmacist or radilologist. Pratically, a vegetable vendor on its stockboard cannot use the word *Solanum melongena* for 'Brinjal. The Jarawas go in sick and come out healthy to live longer and contribute more to their society and their families. For this reason every PHC or hospital is a success story. Every doctor, nurse or lab staff is a life-saver.They can if they want, improve the system which finally could be called the 'Jarawa Specific System'. Such system can be applicable for the non-Jarawas also.

Many dogs are found with Jarawas in their own camps. The Jarawas have started imitating the non-tribals in keeping the dogs as their pets. These dogs are of no help to the Jarawas in their hunting activities but they have become partners to get share of their food. There is imminent danger of outbreak of dangerous disease like rabies. The partaking of food by the dogs may result in shortage of required food for the Jarawas. It is desirable to remove the dogs very carefully without hampering the Jarawa sentiments. Sudden evacuation of the dogs from the Jarawa camps may be resisted by the Jarawas. Interestingly they pick up the stray dogs from the hospital campus and tie them at one corner to take them to home. I was once on a visit to the Jarawa ward at the GB Pant hospital, Port Blair on duty in order to check the attendance of the duty staffs who were deputed there for taking care of the tribal patient. One Jarawa namely Echo with his wife Mono was admitted in the ward for treatment. On my arrival I found two stray dogs tied around his bed with help of a bandage strip. When I tried to persuade the Jarawa to set the dogs free, he turned aggressive which was unexpected to me. After few hours when he went to attend call of nature I forthwith with help of one staff edged a blade on the bandage strip and freed the dogs. I myself had to be invisible for the movement the Jarawa returned and he saw no dog there. It was very difficult moment for me to reduce my laughter at one corner before I returned and asked him – what happened? I must preferably mention here that the Jarawas deliberately never harmed any AAJVS staff in tackling such situation.

As a triggering change in the field of medicinal practice I observed among the Jarwas, they have started to spread the tobacco powder on their wounds and cuts perhaps learnt from the Ranchi poachers.

One of the good things in context of the Jarawa health practices is that they are not interested in smcking in spite of the fact that they are the people who are now trying to copy every thing that we do.

12

Habitat

D.L. Morgan in his description of an encounter with the Jarawas which took place on 26th February, 1918, mentioned the Jarawa village: "The village consisted of 10 huts inhabited by 20 to 30 Jarawas. Each hut was about 3 feet high and 6 feet square. The diametre of the village was about 20 yards. There was thick jungle on all sides, a small nallah running down one side". He said he had been able to destroy two communal huts, but does not specify whether there were any Jarawas inside the huts at the time of destruction. Morgan went on to report - "I came across over 20 old Jarawa villages. Each village had between 7-15 huts. The jungle is full of well beaten tracks. Each of the two communal huts which we destroyed was capable of holding 100 persons. There were several women and children in the village which we raided on the 28th of February. Wherever we found grown-up Jarawa footprints we also found footprints of their children. We recovered a large number of nets and small bows. The nets are made by the Jarawa women, and the small bows are used by the children."

They call their hut as 'Chadda' which is observed to be of different types. A small temporary hut for nuclear family is called 'Tutime-chadda' while their semi-permanent wherein more than 20 Jarawas at a time can live called 'Tohato chadda'. Such types of Chadda was seen on the ATR side near R.K. Nallah in South Andaman for a long time before it was dismantled. Such hut is bee-hive shaped constructed with thatched roof and has few supporting poles inside the hut. The semi-permanent huts can also be seen at Foul Bay, Lakra lungta, Spike Island, Yadita, Chhotalingbang Bay, Jullan Pather and Goal Tekri etc. There is another kind of hut constructed by them called 'Thorkolong chadda'. It was 20th November 2000 when a message received by the office that some Jarwas came to a staging post at Tirur and demanded to board a vehicle to reach the Middle Strait. The task was assigned to me to go and control the situation in the field. I with help of two other assisting staffs somehow persuaded the Jarawas to go back to their hut. They went back to their hut and we too joined them in their journey to the hut called 'Lapaitala' situated in the midst of the forest. It was a semi-permanent community hut inside which we saw about 5-6 healthy Jarawa women. This was the our first official visit to this hut. Some of their chaddas such as Tui chadda, Tuli chadda, Bimu chadda built near the ATR have frequently been visited by the field functionaries and other visitors.

A permanent space is demarcated with help of short poles for each of the families in the community hut which is called 'Thule' in native language. Inside a Jarawa community hut there several separate small hearths can be seen. Inside the hut each hearth (open fire) belongs to each couple or group. But when they have big prey like wild boar or monitor lizard they sit around the big open fire in center of the hut to share the feast. On roof of hut one can witness several bunches of pig-skulls hanging from the roof with help of cane strips. On asking the Jarawa members they stated that every member has separate bunch of skulls of the preys he hunted. It's a matter of pride for them. The huts have proper ventilation horizontally while no way for vertical ventilation. For this reason the hut becomes smoky which causes respiratory problems to the Jarawas. Torka, Keen, Oro and Tulu are the woods/stems used as posts of hut while leaves of Otang, Totanhi, Popo (*Licuala peltata*) and other few trees are used for thatching of the hut. The strips of jungli beth (*Calamus longistus*), pencil beth (*Korthal sialaciniesa*) and mota beth (*Calamus andamanica*) are used to tie the posts. I on all occasions found that their hut is a good abode of flies who cleverely sit at some distance from the fire inside the hut.

Basically the Jarawas construct their community hut near a water source. They do not construct their huts on raised platform but on ground itself. Before the tsunami 2004 I noticed at Jhaokona of Tirur that the forest department had constructed a large temporary hut for sheltering the Jarawas. During my work period I visited many Jarawa huts of different types at different locations and observed that few huts such as Lev chadda, Tui chadda, Tulichadda, Bimu chadda and many others have frequently been used while few huts once or occasionally visited by the semi-nomad natives. Sometimes a temporary hut is identified by name of a person who stays in it. In the year 2000, during the month of December most of the Jarawas were camped at Punnallah for the time being. But one Jarawa family headed by an old man namely Chai was staying with his family near Putatang. The other Jarawas referred to his hut as Chaichadda. This temporary hut was once but for a long time dwelled by Chai and his family members. Similarly one chadda has been named as 'Urpathalai chadda' after a group of girl headed by Urpathale constructed it and stayed for some period.

Earlier the Jarawas used to construct their huts in the dense forests not on the road side. But after their coming into our friendly contact the Jarawas of Boiab (Tirur area), Thidong (Middle Strait area to south of Potatang area but before Punanallah) and Tanmad (the west coast area including the Kekab area) began to construct many huts to stay on the ATR side.

The native names of few identified Jarawa huts are mentioned below.

Boiab: Lapaitala, Eno chadda, Pecheleg chadda, Einaithala chadda, Urpathalai chadda, Hin chadda, Thatahebe chadda, Yonahug chadda, Kihanpo chadda, Mava thute chadda, Maghchap chadda, Muhuthalwa chadda, Hepochitha chadda, Bushu chadda, Hinka chadda, Thoraitha chadda, Wakumthala chadda, Hopenhe chadda, Chipatha chadda, Thotadeve chadda, Holate chadda, Jhaokona chadda, Hukthava chadda, Kehahetai chadda, Anabe chadda, Kunukwa chadda, Hinchaw chadda, Muhaleth chadda, Theetpa chadda, Thonktamade chadda, Alamuhe chadda, Werve chadda, Bimu chadda, Tuli chadda(Punanallah), Thahate chadda and many others. Some other coastal huts are *Koipotale, Ulithotalo, Utalibigiji, Urugyevalui and Olahe.* (The Jarawa names given in this presentation are linguistically yet to be respelled).

Thidong: Motebute chadda, Tuluga chadda, Hotokunu chadda, Tuhi chadda(RK Nallah), Labeta chadda, Tuterbelo chadda, Mimun chadda, Katabobo chadda and many others.

Tanmad: Levchadda(Dhaninallah), Tanmad, Oney chadda(Lakralungta), Hulele chadda, Ulli chadda and Tharmachadda(Spike Island), Motiete chadda (Foul Bay) and many others.

The Jarawas construct their huts chiefly in bank of creek, near sea, deep forests and peripheral forests on ATR sides. The natives have exceptional indigenous knowledge about their forests and forest types or we can say 'homes' or 'types of homes'. Most of the trees they identify by just looking at the tree trunk while in their company sometimes I had to look at the top canopy to identify the tree. The Jarawa territory is luxuriant with various types of rainforests such as–1) The giant evergreen forests, 2) The tropical evergreen forest, 3) The hill top tropical evergreen forests, 4) The semi-evergreen forests, 5) The moist deciduous forests, 6) The Littoral forests and 7) The mangrove vegetations. The Giant evergreen forests generally develop near banks of streams where soils are deep and alluvial. The main trees of this type of forests are Gurjan, *Callophyllum soulattri* (Poon), Artocarpus chaplasa (*Taung pienne*), Lamba patti, Amoora wallichii (Lalchini) and Sterculia campanulata (Papita), etc. The tropical evergreen forest can be noticed at a hill with little slope with Gurjan, Kala Lakuch, Poon, red bombway (*Panchionia andamanica*), Thingam, Bakota, Khattaphal and Jaiphal etc. The hill top tropical evergreen forests grow on hill tops and sometimes on steep slopes lower down on poorer soils. These are Gurjan, Mesuaferrea, Hopea belferi and Euphorbia trigona etc which are usually exposed to high winds and trees are somewhat stunted in growth. The semi-evergreen forests include giant trees both deciduous and evergreen occurring mainly on drained soils and tableland are Gurjan, Letkok, White chuglam, White bombway, *Pterocarpus dalbergioides* (Padauk), Pynma, Bonmeza, Albizzia lebbek (Koko) and Didu etc. The moist deciduous forests are formed by giant trees of about 40 meters high, 3 meters in girth and heavily buttressed. They generally occur on hill areas but not exceeding beyond 75-100 meters altitude. They are Padauk, *Diospyros marmorata* (Marble wood), *Sagerea elliptica* (Chooi), White dhoop and Koko etc. The littoral forests formed by Mimusops, Littoralis (Bullet wood), Thitpok and Badam etc. commonly develop on a high level soil along the coast line but beyond the reach of tidal waters. The mangrove vegetations occupy extensively the shores, mouth of creeks, and inland channels etc.

The fading of local knowledge of forests among the Jarawa's young members through its interaction with the dominant our knowledge, takes place at many levels through many steps. Now our knowledge has generally been viewed by them as universal because the knowledge and power nexus is inherent in our dominant system. Orthodoxically to us their knowledge system is closed to our doubts, our scrutiny and evaluation. This may disturb and destroy the Jarawa knowledge of reality. Some forest dwellers gather food directly from the forest, while many communities practise agriculture outside the forest, but depend on the fertility of the forest. In our so-called scientific but dominant knowledge system which splits forestry from agriculture and reduces forestry to timber and wood supply, food is no longer a category related to forestry. The Jarawa knowledge of food forestry at one stage in future may be erased. According to a study, Dominant forestry science has no place for the knowledge of the Hanunoo in the Philippines who divide plants into 1,600 categories, of which trained botanists can distinguish only 1,200. Similarly the knowledge base of the cropping systems based on 160 crops of the Lua tribe in Thailand is taken as knowledge. A recent study of the experts on a high court guideline on the Jarawas revealed that the tribals have a distinct and workable knowledge about their forests. To us, what do the forests bear? Medicine, resin and timber. But ask to them and they will say — Food, water and pure air.

The India's *Chipko* and *Appiko Movements* are movements of agricultural communities against the destruction of the forests that support agriculture. The timber blockades of the Penan and other tribes of Sarawak are signs of struggles of forest peoples against systems of forest management which destroy the forest and its people. The Andaman rainforests are being destroyed because the value of rainforest land is perceived as only the value of its timbers. The scale of human pressures on rainforests' ecosystems has increased enormously in the last few decades. Nearly half of the species of plants, animals and microorganisms will be destroyed or severely threatened over the next quarter century due to rainforest deforestation leading to the loss of Jarawa, if no preventive measure at warfoot level is undertaken. In Africa alone, the colonists have destroyed more than 100 indigenous tribes since the 1900's. With them centuries of accumulated knowledge of the medicinal value of rainforest species have gone. When a senior Jarawa dies without passing his arts on to the next generation, the tribe and the world loses an ancient and irreplaceable knowledge about the medicinal plants.

13

The Life Cycle Rituals

All important event of a life cycle is celebrated with dance and songs among the Jarawas. Remarkably, they are incredibly creative in their songs. From my Diary Note dated 23-08-2005 "...Today one healthy male child was born at RK Nallah. When myself and my staffs visited their hut few Jarawas were singing songs being paused in the interims. As soon as they they saw us they changed their lyrics (but not the rythm) which we interpreted as '..Charkar Babu (Me)..Yadav (my staff) came to see the child but did not bring 'Dabadaba' (biscuit) and Kangapo (clothes)...and they say 'Lep allema nadem' (don't come on road)... #!@?*# (abusive words to us in fun).. they don't give us Dabadaba..and Kangapo... today we shall hunt crab and tomorrow Dabadaba will come...but kangapo will not come....". We guessed that in lieu of his offer of crab to a traveler he will surely get biscuits on next day; but usually the tavellers do not give clothes to them..". Such type of song (Gegabe) is sung only for fun by the Jarawas particularly when they are in a vehicle heading to their habitat after being discharged from a PHC or hospital. On such occasions their songs, mixed with shouts becoming cacophony of joy, are devoted to the driver and the staffs escorting them. They are really very funny people. But their lyrics in general revolve around the natural objects like sea, sand, sun, moon, wind, tree, pig, and the supernatural powers. Their dances are extremely simple with minimum of steps or movement. Some of the dances are performed with rhythmic clapping and/or stepings. Men and women perform some dances exclusively. On most of the occasions, the dancers sing themselves, and like 'Bomu' of the Great Andamanese they don't have any musical instrument. Almost, all the tribal communities of the world have music and dance to communicate and to express their spiritual beliefs. For example, the Great Andamanese of Andaman islands perform 'Bomu dance' beating a piece of wood called 'Bomu' in their marriages and other celebrations. The Bushman of Kalahari desert in South Africa perform dance to summon up the power for healing rituals. The Hopi tribal members of south-west parts of USA sing and celebrate to bring rain. Such examples may never end if we travel every part of the world.

For marriages in the Jarawa society I observed two different cases of selecting partners. In first case, the boy and girl make love in forests before marriage hiding all eyes. In the second case, the boy and girl are paired by their parents with consent of both the sides and before that they never had any love affair. Quite often it was observed that when young and teenaged girls engage themselves in forest in collection of food, the Jarawa boys chase them and make sexual intercourse with them. Especially I noticed this at Boiab (Tirur). There, to escape themselves from the boys the girls in a group made their hideouts in the adjacent paddy fields of the local settlers and on many occassions came to the Jawara Protection Police (JPP) Camp at Tirur No 4. The other Jarawa members or group never came forward to protect them. But I must mention that the Tirur girls are not alone neglected and raped so openly. From our own general social views and opinions about the social cruelties, we find that the Jarawas are not so cruel or violent comparing to many other tribal communities of the world. In Africa, Papua New Guinea, Australia and other tribal areas the girls are often neglected, raped and tortured in more hostile forms. In African tribes mothers, not men, insist on chopping off their daughters' genitals, producing "horrendous pain, massive bleeding and raging infection." It currently is in many African countries including Sudanese women and in large number of uneducated Egyptian families. It began historically thousands of years ago before the nations became Muslim, so it is not caused by Islamic beliefs. "Girls tremble as they hear about the experiences of other girls...first there is fear, and then the appalling memory of the experience. Some girls live with a phobia that one or the other day parent will kill them. But such way of brutal torturing of girls I never saw among the Jarawas.The mainstream Jarawas still do not allow the outsiders to the possible extent to attend their rituals except the AAJVS functionaries. The Jarawas are strictly monogamous. Usually the parents of a child or elder persons of the family start discussing a match for marriage, when the prospective bride or groom is one or two years old. On many occasions such marriages are not finally solomnised.

Generally, clear consent of both the bride and groom is received before solemnizing a marriage. Marriage in kinship is strictly prohibited. A boy cannot marry with his sister (waami) and cousins like father's sister's daughter, father's brother's daughter, mother's sister's daughter and mother's brother's daughter. Among them the inter- territorial marriages are commonly solemnized. The community members do allow re- marriage of a widow or widower in general conditions. In many cases I noticed a wide age gap between such couples. Their marriage ceremony is very simple. The elders surround the groom and bride who then sit in the centre. After a while both the boy and girl sit in the laps of all the senior relatives one after another. After that the boy sits again in the centre with his legs straight. Then the girl sits in his lap and the boy hugs her for a while. The way she sits in the lap of her partner I observed in the same manner among the Onges of Dugong Creek when I conducted historical re-marriages of four Onge widows viz Champa,28 (paired with Kwakui 28), Reetai,23 (paired with Santosh 23), Tikoigagae,31 (paired with Uglai 31), and Shanti,25 (paired with Koitangae 25) on 16 th January 2009 being in charge of their settlement. I causiously paired them in accordance with their cultural rules that the inter- band marriages and widow marriages are allowed in the Onge society. In the Jarawa marriage the pork as feast is served to all the members. Such ceremony is incomplete if pork is not offered as feast. The Onges after their resettlement do not find pig easily in their forest, due to which no 'Tanagiru ceremony' has been performed for a long time. In the 'Tangiru' about 21 pigs are required to be hunted rirually. They sing and dance in joy and happiness. This time they do not try to corrupt/ edit the conventional lyrics while singing a song. After this point of time they become a new family which is the smallest demographic unit of the Jarawa society. I noticed that the Jarawa marriages take place mostly between the Middle Andaman group and RK Nallah group and between the Tirur group and the Putatang or RK Nallah group because of the territorial closeness. Very rarely marriages occurred between Tirur and Middle Andaman group because of the territorial restrain. After the marriage the new family initially prefers to stay out of the group to spend newly married life which we say in our words 'the Honeymoon period'. They camp in forest and construct a new family hut. They take shelter in community hut especially in rainy season. Significantly they in all walks of life when need help, their relatives come forward and help them. The endogamous Jarawas believe that if any member becomes responsible for damaging a married life the spirits punish him and he becomes a bald one. During her pregnancy the girl is restricted to eat some wild fruits and tubers. The old Jarawas constantly warn the girl in pregnancy to avoid alien foods like biscuit, rice, bread, chocolate, pan, tobacco, and honey and some wild roots and tubers which may cause abortion. Sometimes when the girl demands little honey is given to her but she is not allowed to touch the honey. Her husband or sister feeds her through their hands. Some other food items such as larvae of insects, crab, monitor lizard, and few wild fruits are also restricted to her. She is offered pork, fish, turtle, turtle eggs, and a wild tuber called 'Jyev' in their language. They believe that the 'Jyev' increases blood level which helps the woman to be physically strong. They have a very special 'Jyev song' I enjoyed on many occasions. The wild 'Umin' is believed to be dangerous if eaten by a pregnant woman. They believe that the size of the embryo increases to give painful birth if 'Umin' is consumed during pregnancy. The pork is eaten without fear and after eating it the pregnant woman decorates her abdomen with the great care with white clay. The delivery of the child is generally attended by some senior women of the community while men stand at a corner or out of the hut to avoid seeing the delivery. The umbilical cord is carefully cut with help of their traditional knife 'Towa'. They wrap the placenta 'Enaipak' with help of some leaves and hang it on a tree at a distance in forest. The mother after delivery of child is given complete rest for next few days. She lactates her new born baby till the dental formation of the child but after 6-8 months in addition to the mother's milk (colostrums) the infant is given little water, little fat of pig and little honey. The little baby is not only taken care by the parents but also by other relatives and teenaged boys and girls of the group. Some other women also feed the baby if felt essential. The baby is massaged by using fat of monitor lizard especially during cold (Anyame). The baby is caressed, kissed, hugged and carried by the elders on their backs with help of bark strips. After few years the child does not sleep with his/her mother and father in their space. He/she starts spending time mostly with the children of the same age group. I feel that these children really spend their childhood absolutely in the lapse of mother nature. They play game of collecting tiny fishes in shallow water, go to hunt mud crab in marsh, accompany the women engaged in collection of fruits and tubers in forests and they sometimes play with toy bows and arrows targeting birds and fruits with great competition among them. Gradually the child grows up and attains adolescence through some rituals.

A boy is considered to be a matured man only after he killed a pig with no help of others. He goes through a ritual called 'Lepa'. As per the 'Lepa' ritual after killing of a pig the man is given a new name. He brings the pig to his hut and gives to his mother or sister or in absence of both to a cousin. He is then made to sit with folded legs on the back of hunted pig, his first prey and at the moment the senior members sing the Lepa songs. After a while he is forced to dance with other male members. After the dance, he sits on the lap of the person to whom he gave the pig. The pig after coking in first of all is given to him to eat. After eating the pork the pig fat is massaged on the body of the new Lepa. Surprisingly he is joyously forced to over eat the pork. In the end he vomits and goes to sleep. Our surprise does not end here. On the next morning singing and dancing continues. Not in anger but ritually the adult members of the hut throw all the commodities out of the hut. Ultimately the situation becomes normal and the boy becomes a normal Lepa like others. For the Jarawas, Lepa is more important ritual than any other ritual. With emergence of new Lepa, their number of hunters is increased. If they have good number of hunters in their group, they can never go empty stomach. In the month of December 2008, With the death of 06 adult Onges out of 08 viz. Bulambegi, Kimboi, Anil, Teetu, Chotaraju, Bairogagae due to consumption of a poisonous liquid, the Onges of Dugong Creek irrepairably lost their hunters. Looking to such critical condition of the group, the other groups of Onge (groups of

Jackson Creek and South Bay) allowed few of their young hunters to be adopted by the bereaved group (Dugong Creek group). 'Lepa' is much joyous and very important for them, because, to them, 'living' is more important than anything else.

In the Jarawa society simple temporary restrictions can be observed when a girl attains her first menstruation. To them the menstruation is a physiological process often imbued with their culture and some traditional beliefs. However, not all societies have interpreted menstruation in the same way: in some cultures it has been perceived as relatively unimportant, subject to neither stigma nor taboo; in others, menstruation has been a sign of the magical power of the female body, in all its mysterious fecundity. Indeed many societies exhibit profound ambivalence where menstruation is concerned, imbuing it with both positive and negative meanings, making it difficult to arrive at a single interpretation of menstrual taboos. According to the ancient medical writers the menstrual blood constitutes a toxic substance that need to purge itself from the body. On attaining menarche called 'Doile' the girl sleeps straight on the licuala leaves underneath of which there is a carpet of stem of jungle supari (wild arecanut). The 'Doile' songs are sung by some members and the dance is performed by a group. The Doile is celebrated joyously by the female members comparing to the male members. Remarkably when the girl sits for a while her head is waved horizontally on both the directions. On her first menstruation, the girl sits at a corner being segregated from others. The male members make a platform of bamboo or planks of wild arecanut (Areca triandra) or other wood on which Licuala leaves or leaves of another variety called 'Dou' are spread for her to sit comfortably over it. Sometimes a special variety of leaves which look large and round are used in place of the Licuala leaves. She is not allowed to sleep with her husband during the first few days of her menstruation. One day I observed that an unmarried girl during her menstruation period went to the forest with few other girls of the same age group to collect 'Keen', an edible wild fruit. She was made to sit underneath a tree on carpet of some jungle haldi (wild turmeric) leaves. The other girls collected the fruit and sat near to her. They together relished the fruit. To my understanding, such practise is not of the Jarawa mainstream. As observed on many occasions, a woman being evacuated to nearest primary health centre by our office jeep even in her menstruation period sat with other members of the family in the rear seat. But it was noticeable that she put some leaves of Pterospermum acerifolium over the seat and then she sat on it. Nobody of the community was reluctant in sending her with us. Thus, the Jarawas have ritual restrictions but also allow the situational relaxations.

Sometimes the Jarawas have shown great negligence in taking care of their orphans. Years ago one Jarawa boy aged 5 or 6 years namely 'Tangato' was found neglected and injured on ATR side. He was pushed to a hearth. Immediately he was brought under medical treatment. The further investigation revealed that this Jarawa boy was an orphan and living in great negligence among the Jarawas. After an enquiry we found that there was a maternal uncle of the boy namely Noru. He was further successfully persuaded to accept the boy and take care of him.

Death is said to be the physical end of a life on this earth. In the Jarawa society the death can be divided into three viz. Natural death, the Unnatural or Accidental death and the Ooper chadda death. When a man dies, his widow cries and observes the mourning period for several days. She sits at one corner and talks very little. The Jarawas do not bury their dead, while Onge and Great Andamanese bury their dead. When a child is dead, a single man of the group takes the body to deep forest and nobody dares to accompany him in his further journey into the forest. After a while he returns back with his hands empty. When I brought Tahechu's dead child (died in the GB Pant hospital at Port Blair) into her habitat at Punanallah, the maternal uncle of the child namely 'Gena' took the body to the forest and after a while he returned back with empty hands. Similarly on 12/03/2005 morning a Jarawa female child namely Ekopathai Tuithi D/o Veketa was died at GB Pant Hospital, Port Blair and on the same day we brought the body of the deceased to Punanallah at around 03:00 PM. One man said to be his maternal uncle offered the dead to the densed forest. As per the Jarawa say, the dead child after his death goes to the sky with ankane (a supernatural soul who takes the dead) a benevolent spirit. When an adult is dead, the corpse is placed between two buttresses of a single tree (thodkitoo). Then plenty of leaves are thrown therein to cover the dead and the bereaved members apply red clay (Alame) on their hands and faces and leave the place for one or few months. The members present in the hut also do the same. They sing in memory of the deceased person. Once I joined them while keeping the corpse between the buttresses. The bereaved members smeared red clay on my forehead, cheek, arms and legs and requested me not to tell anybody about the place. They hide this matter only for the reason that after few months they will come back here and take out the small bones of the dead. Among the Onges once I observed that in the death ritual called 'Enibirangae' the cheek bone was taken out of the grave and given to 'Obiyutebe' (who wears the bone) and all other Onges smeared red clay on their bodies. But my this observation differed from other death observations. Obviously they have situational/conditional practices. The Jarawas have been found to wear small lower jawbones or clavical bones or other small bones of the deceased around the neck or around the waist to attain the quality and power of the decesaed. After the burial ritual completed in all respects they leave the hut if the death occurred therein. In case of the death of

Tahechu's child they did not leave the hut because the death occurred in a hospital. After the death when for the first time a pig is hunted, the widow with her companions bow down to the pig or hug it and cries loudly in memory of her husband. On an occasion I asked from a Jarawa man, why she cried on the pig? Her husband is not here to eat the pig meat, he replied. The widow does the same when any turtle is hunted for the first time. Similarly a widower weeps at first hunted pig or turtle in memory of his beloved wife. The widower while collecting honey from a tree for the first time after death of his wife he cries loudly sitting in the tree branch. At this moment one can observe how emotional they are. Most importantly it is to mention that for the Jarawas death is only of the body and the soul never dies which sits absolutely fit to our spiritual belief about the body and soul. To them a soul after death of the body reaches the Ooper chadda (Sky abode) to stay with the ancestors in happiness. Inspite of our several attempts to unfold their myths and actual practices pertaining to their 'Ooper chadda' the knowledge we attained hitherto is still insatiable. The 'Ooper' is a Hindi word for 'Pangne' (Sky) pronounced by the Jarawas themselves perhaps for our better understanding. The Jarawas never took us to the place in the forest where as they said they performed Ooper chadda death practice. And we never tried to see the spot with the fear of Jarawa aggressiveness. Our religious concept of paradise exists a bit near to their explaination about the Ooper chadda. They believe that after the death their member (soul) directly goes to the sky abode called 'Ooper chadda' and live with their ancestors in happiness. They enjoy pig, honey, fishes and water in the Ooper chadda. The Jarawas told me that some of their senior living members make occasional visit to the Ooper chadda to meet the forefathers but nobody saw them while going there. The man who wants to visit the Ooper chadda enters the deep forest and stand with one leg folded and summon the ancestral souls to pull him up. The natives were never able to tell me what happens after that. Not to them but to me the saddest aspect of the Jarawa society is that they killed many living children in their practices of the Ooper chadda. Many children when became seriously sick, they were shown the way of Ooper chadda. It was also observed that when the Jarawas see a child sick and near to death, they take the sick child to the forest and send them (kill them) to the Ooper chadda. A child born after the death of father or if given birth by an unmarried girl is declared 'illegal'. Such child is often killed in their practices of Ooper chadda. If we take a look into the cases and practices of child killings nearing the 'Ooper Chadda' concept in other tribal cultures then we find that in many of the tribal societies the childhood is just a war against 'unnatural death'. The practice of killing children is prevalent among several tribal communities of the present world. Many anthropologists have written extensively about killing of children in tribal cultures. For example - Infanticide rates were enormous in New Guinea, with the first missionaries estimating that two-thirds of the children were murdered by their parents. As in other tribal cultures, abstinence and abortion were well known, but infanticidal practice was common. The growing children were routinely traumatized while they watched their mothers strangle or otherwise murder their siblings. Similar to that of the Jarawas, they throw away their infants not because of lack of resources to feed them. For them (Not Jarawa) the demon children are killed. The living children watch their mothers bury their siblings live, eat them, or toss them to sow to devour. Some tribes kill so many newborn that they regularly have to buy children from neighboring tribes so their tribe won't disappear. Females in New Guinea are treated brutally. Most of the children are malnourished in New Guinea, studies show, even when food is plentiful, because mothers only feed them a couple of times a day, and they die from starvation while the mothers are puzzled what is wrong with them. In New Guinea a mother chokes the infant with her milk during nursing. In another tribal culture eating 'every second child' and making the older children also eat them have also been reported. Mothers regularly forced their children to eat their newborn siblings with the belief that the strength of the first child would be doubled by such a procedure. Sometimes the fetus would be "pulled out by the head, roasted and eaten by the mother and the children" and sometimes "a big boy would be killed by the father by being beaten on the head" and given to the mother to eat. The mutilation of young girls' vaginas is also practiced by the tribes, in which old men roll feathers with a loop of hair. This device is put into the vagina and then removed, pulling away a large part of the womb. The rest of the womb is then cut horizontally and vertically with a stone knife. When this wound is healed, the girl is then circumcised and made to have intercourse with many young men. The mix of blood and semen is collected and given to frail tribesmen as a fortifying elixir. Males marry many wives and even rape their own daughters in order to fortify their masculinity. Most African tribal mothers still kill at least one of their children, sometimes as a child sacrifice to the gods. Infanticide of course is a routine practice in African tribes, as in tribal cultures around the world, with more girls than boys killed at birth. In view of this horrible scenario we may say that the Andaman tribes including the Jarawas have no such violant practices among themselves. They do not concentrate on the killing of girl child. The practices of the circumcision, cannibalism and other abusive practices are absolutely absent in the Jarawa society. In my opinion, the Jarawas if compared to the other tribes as mentioned above are much sensible and humanitarians. They kiss on the forehead of the infant, hug them and carry them on back while working. They name their babies quite affectionately.

My main purpose behind reproducing briefly the examples of child killing and other hostile rituals in other tribal cultures is to prove that the child killing in the Jarawa society is neither new to the present world of tribes nor so thickly practiced. We realize that the Jarawas have something embedded and hidden in their culture and beliefs in context of their child killing in the name of the 'Ooper chadda'. Not withstanding the said Papuans and other tribal communities, on one hand the Jarawas kill their children in the name of 'Ooper chadda' while on the other hand as observed they have great feelings of love for their children. The child adoption is also practiced apart from the fact that few small girls left neglected in the Tirur area. Inspired by the socio-cultural norms of other tribes, the answer to why the Jarawa girls roam in neglected conditions at Tirur can now be discovered to be 'a normal fact' of them.

As far as 'the care for old persons' is concerned I observed that the Jarawas do avoid taking old men with them in their journey of long walk. But they never do the things as the other tribes do. In certain savage tribes in Papua New Guinea, they put the old people up in the trees and shake them once a year in the spring; if they don't fall down they let them live another year.

The Jarawas live in complete harmony with the mother nature. All parts of their routine activities and rituals from birth to death are absolutely and undoubtedly eco-friendly.

14

Cultural Anthroponomy

The indigenous method of naming the children is an important part of the cultural anthroponomy of the Jarawa society. One Jarawa member gets an opportunity to change his name through the ritual of adolescence/adulthood. Traditionally among the Andaman negritos the anthroponomy is based on names of the objects of nature, traditional art and artifacts.

In short anthoponomy of any group can be considered as the reflective codes of their ethno-semantic, eco-cultural socio-political or religious reality. Hence it may be defined as political codes too. Like others the Onges, the Great Andamanese and the Jarawa also have a unique system of personal names which are constructed according to linguistic rules of their languages. Their anthroponomy is eco-cultural in nature i.e personal nomenclature among them is derived from their ecological association to nature. The forest nurtured an ecological civilization and their personal names had been derived from such a fraternity to nature, plants, animals, sun, wind, stone, clay, time, place, occupational context, food articles, festivals etc. Each of them is the nucleus of their anthroponomy.

Equivalent Meaning of some Onge and Jarawa words

Sl. No.	*Onge Word*	*Jarawa Word*	*Meaning*
1.	Thiranange	Thala	Papaya
2.	Ikulukutu	Hulu	Heat
3.	Alahuwa	Ahuwai	Telling lie
4.	Miyasheka	Miyash	forgotten
5.	Enghe	Engh	Water
6.	Narema	Nadem	No
7.	Gatibe	Atiba	Name
8.	Me eyekota	Whammy eyekota	Sister
9.	Khuwe/Tamanua	Wuwe	Pig
10.	Wome/Kuve	Wome	Dog
11.	Buchu	Busu	Cooking Vessel
12.	Aale	Echele	Small child
13.	Pechame	Pechame	Died
14.	Enen	Enen	Outsider
15.	Phonei	Phonei	Light
16.	Tukhe	Tuhe	Fire
17.	Koilabo	Kangapo	Cloth
18.	Aa	Aaw	Bow
19.	Enikwe	Enikwa	Ear
20.	Enichipu	Enichipu	Eye
21.	Gigawawe	Gigabe	Song
22.	Wanabe	Whana	To cry
23.	Enhiwe	Enchiye	To laugh
24.	Whe	Whod	Soil
25.	Wene	Wene	Digging rod
26.	Haniranagae	Hiniwe	Stomach
29.	Yono	Yono	Neighbouring negritos
30.	Eurugye	Eurugye	Crocodile

Now it is feared that the traditional naming may be obsolete in the new generation of the Jarawa. Instead of their own names many alien names such as Raja, Mary, etc. have now infiltrated among them. Though fashions in names in all languages of the world have undergone changes in the course of history, one cannot conclude such changes in the Jarawa context simply either as acculturation or development or as the Jarawa realization to adopt new names.

The practice of nominalization among the Onges, based on the nature culture objects & cultural practices, is being added by the modernized nominalization. The names among the Onges such as Ramesh, Suresh, Indira, Santosh, Kanchan, Rakesh, Jain, Vicky, Kavita, Rajni, BadaRaju, Mausami, Anuradha, Shekhar, Meena kumari, Maya, Champa, Prashant, Bharat, Sheela, Rajkumar, Shanti, Meena Kumari, Madan, Arati, Priya, Sarlina, Radhika, Bharati, Mukesh, Palith, Jyoti, Raja, Ronny, Shiva, Tulsi, Dilip, Ujala, etc. reveal that there has been a great change in the cultural practice of nominalization among the Onges. Nominalization among the Onges has also been unauthorisedly practiced or we may say UNWANTED INTERFERRENCE IN ONGE ANTHROPONOMY by the medical staffs, nurses, office staff & other non-Onges. With the passage of time as result of the frequent contacts this may also happen among the Jarawas. The Jarawas in their mainstream still name themselves in their orthodox manner. For example : Alutai (F), Taichu (F), Tataha (M), Ingana (M), Gillet (M), Otteha (M), Kehawai (M), Ullegad (M), Thahati (F), Atiunase (F), Tepohane(M), Tawaitolaye(F), Lapa (F), Lipu-ane (Bindu) (F), Enopahiley (F), Urpathaley (F), Uko-ela (F), Lole (F), Youkta (F), Eno-pahi-le (F), Baliabe (F), Kuku-we (F), Minodili (F), Tole (F), Thorawethal (F), Hue-tai (F), Chadu (F), Tawaihone (F), Aninja (F), Tenyaho (F), Tawetaja (F), Himounda (M), Annamalai (M), Majiammu (M), Ujagle (M), Eling (M), Dagabai (M), Vada (M); Kunu

(M), Tuithi (M), Thada (M), Thadu (F), Obisey (F), Atela (M), Tativannaelahaney (F), Mahe (M), Laha (M), Tatiwanayelonganey (F), Inoyenja (M), Thorwabeyal (F), Gena (M), Thetha (F), Thegathiga (F), Anjale (M), Thenyawa (F), Inahleha (M), Yumu (M), Achehane (M), Theaab (M), Tapvan (F), Tatiye (M), Eebe (F), Thodoya (M), Yachuin (F), Kuyab (F), Ashu (M), Yethineanche (M), Yethayepohane (M), Aybye (F), Towetetebenehene (M), Tangnawaleho (M), Yepayume (F), Echo (M), Mono (F), Tativathab Tetvine (M), Leva (M), Thabane (F), Yelagagetho (M), Jomo (F), Kange (M), Borvo (F), Napoji (M), Totopal (F), Thivathe (M), Sapale (F), Thototerovat (M), Kaham (M), Bekachi (F), Chaithoune (F), Othagna (M), Tathivatantakhahe (M), Thopo (M), Kuhoya (F), Puchutava (M), Nachaaa (F), Taji (F), Mana (F), Ahela (F), Hotta (M), Aiobiyavey (M), Teetapa (M), Thaichepale (F), Tangna (M), Ugotailing (M), Chitto (M), Somolo (F), Shanbabu (M), Ekagna (M), Chohaparani (F), Atbo (M), Tanganam (M), Wahala (F), Sankakta (M), Lahale (M), Enmen (M), Hane (F), Malawate (F), Puhu (M), Theogem (F), Chapale (M), Bithal (M), Itaidekcho (F), Momo (M), Uga (F), Thiyale (F), Chaho (M), Aagko (M), Veketa (M), Thabote (F), Epinume (F), Ennathe (M), Chelo (F), Thawai (M), Barale (F), Chatuetho (M), Tomu (M), Thabateba (M), Lyalihe (M), Teyathahe (M), Hulu (F), Ledha (M), Etimo (F), Aggathy (M), Thoya (Majikwa) (M), Thaiyab (F), Betha (M), etc.

It was observed that the Onges are not capable of pronouncing properly most of the names given by the non-Onges to them. For example Kavita is pronouncd as Kapita, Jain as Chayan, Champa as Sampa, Prashant as Prachant, Bharat as Barat, Shekhar as Chekar.

It is interesting to say that the alien name Kavita has altered to Kapita by the Onges. This sound alteration 'V>P' shows their acquaintance with phoneme /p/ especially in the context of complete absence of /v/. Hence it may be concluded positively that Brown's observation of 'P' was right or it may be due to the effects of transplanted /p/ by reflexification. Similarly the Jarawas never pronounced me as SIRCAR/ SARKAR but 'Chakar Babu' and they are aware of their ability and inability in their pronouncing words and accordingly they name their children.

Earlier the Andamanese gave names to their children while they were in the wombs. After the child was born another name was added indicating weather the child was male or female. Women were given flower names also. This was done at the time of menstruation, and the young girls were given the names of the flowers of whichever trees happened to be in bloom at the time.

I am of firm belief that the tribals should be left free to name their babies as they like. Change of name does not signify development; instead it may hurt the Jarawa sentiments.

Bibliography

Administration Reports.

Andaman Adim Janjati Vikas Samiti, Retrieval from Precipice, Port Blair, 1977.

Andaman and Nicobar Administration, Gazetteers.

Andaman & Nicobar Manuals.

Awaradi,S.A, Master Plan, 1991

Forest Administration Report (1901-02).

Kalpavriksh, *Ravaged Forests and Soiled Seas*, New Delhi, 1989.

Mukhopadhyay, K. (et al.): *Jarawa Contact: Ours With Them Theirs With Us*, Anthropological Survey of India, Kolkata, 2002.

Naidu, S.P.P.K, *Andaman Chronicles*, Phenomenon Publication, Port Blair, 2003.

Sircar, P.K, *The Primitive Tribes of Andaman & Nicobar Islands*, Akansha Publishing House, New Delhi, 2004.

The Andaman Express, Port Blair

The Aspect, Port Blair

The Daily Telegrams, Port Blair.

The Hindu, Chennai

The Light of Andamans, Port Blair.

UNESCO.2010. The Jarawa Tribal Reserve Dossier: Cultural & Biological Diversities in the Andaman Islands. Edited by Pankaj Sekhsaria and Vishvajit Pandya 212 pp. Paris: UNESCO.

www. psychohistory.com

www. andaman.org

www.and.nic.in

www.survival-international.org.

and Others

ANNEXURE I

The Andaman and Nicobar Islands (Protection of Aboriginal Tribes) Regulation, 1956

(Published by Authority on Saturday, 30 June 1956)

Notification

Port Blair, 18 June 1956

No 76/56: The following Regulation promulgated under clause (2) of article 243 of the constitution and published in the Gazette of India, Extraordinary, Part II, Section I, dated the 14th May 1956 is republished here for general information.

The Andaman and Nicobar Islands (Protection of Aboriginal Tribes) Regulation(ANPATR), 1956*

No.3 of 1956: Promulgated by the President in the seventh year of the Republic of India. A regulation to provide for the protection of the interests of socially and economically backward aboriginal tribes in the Andaman and Nicobar Islands. In exercise of the powers conferred by clause (2) of article 243 of the constitution, the President is pleased to promulgate the following Regulation made by him.

1. This Regulation may be called the Andaman and Nicobar Islands (Protection of Aboriginal Tribes) Regulation, 1956.

   (2) It extends to the whole of the Andaman and Nicobar Islands.

   (3) It shall come into force on such date as the Chief Commissioner may by notification appoint.

2. In this Regulation, unless the context otherwise requires:

   (a) 'aboriginal tribe' means any of the following tribes or tribal communities in the Andaman and Nicobar Islands, and includes parts of, or groups within, such tribes or tribal communities, namely: Andamanese, Jarawas, Onges, Sentinelese, Nicobarese, and Shompens;

(b) 'Chief Commiossioner' means the Chief Commissioner of the Andaman and Nicobar Islands;

(c) 'Deputy Commissioner' means Deputy Commissioner of the Andaman and Nicobar Islands;

(d) 'notification' means a notification published in the Official Gazette;

(e) 'pass' means a pass granted under section 7; and,

(f) 'reserve area' means an area which the Chief Commissioner has, by notification under section 3, declared to be a reserved area.

3. (1) The Chief Commissioner may, by notification, declare any area which is predominantly inhabited by aboriginal tribes to be reserved area and specify the limits of such area; and may, from time to time, in like manner, alter such limits.

(2) If any question arises whether any falls within or without a reserved area, it shall be decided by the Chief Commissioner and his decision shall be final.

4. No waste or unoccupied land at the disposal of the Government in a reserved area shall be allotted for agricultural purposes to any person other than a member of an aboriginal tribe:

Provided that the Chief Commissioner may allot any such land to any person other than a member of an aboriginal tribe-

(a) If the Chief Commissioner is satisfied that such land is not required by any such member; or

(b) If in his opinion the allotment of land to a person other than a member of an aboriginal tribe is necessary for the purpose of consolidation of land or is otherwise in the public interest.

5. (1) No member of an aboriginal tribe shall, except with the previous sanction of the Chief Commissioner, transfer by way of sale, exchange mortage, lease or otherwise any land to any person other than a member of an aboriginal tribe.

(2) No land held or occupied by a member of an aboriginal tribe shall be liable to attachment or sale in execution of any decree or order of a civil or revenue court.

(3) Any transfer, attachment or sale of any land made in contravention of this section shall be void.

6. (1) No person other than a member of an aboriginal tribe shall, except with the previous sanction of the Chief Commissioner, acquire any interest in any land situated in any reserved area or in any product of, or crop raised on, such land, or shall, except under and in accordance with the terms and conditions of a licence granted by the Chief Commissioner, carry on any trade or business in such area.

(2) The provisions of sub-section (1) shall apply to any person who, at the commencement of this regulation, is carrying on any trade or business in any such area after the expiration of 60 days from such commencement.

7. The Chief Commissioner may, by notification, prohibit any person other than a member of an aboriginal

tribe or any class of persons other than member of an aboriginal tribe from entering a reserved area except on the authority and subject to the observance of the conditions and restrictions of a pass granted by the Deputy Commissioner or by such other officers as the Deputy Commissioner may authorise in writing in this behalf.

8. (1) Whoever in contravention of the provisions of section 6, acquires any interest in or in any product of, or crop raised on, any land, or carries on any trade or business, in a reserved area, shall be punishable with imprisonment which may extend to one year or with fine which extend to one thousand rupees, or with both; and the interest so acquired shall be disposed of in such manner as the Chief Commissioner may, after taking into consideration the circumstances of the case, direct.

(2) Whoever, in contravention of the notification issued under section 7, enters a reserved area shall be punishable with imprisonment which may extend to one year, or with fine which may extend to one thousand rupees or with both.

(3) Whoever, does anything in contravention of any of the conditions or restrictions subject to which a pass has been granted to him under section 7, shall be punishable with imprisonment which may extend to one year, or with fine which may extend to one thousand rupees or with both.

9. (1) The Chief Commissioner, or any person authorised by him in this behalf may arrest without a warrant any person who has committed, or is suspected of having committed, any offence punishable under this regulation.

(2) Every person arrested under sub-section (1) shall be produced before the nearest magistrate within twenty four hours of such arrest excluding the time necessary for the journey from the place of arrest.

10. (1) The Chief Commissioner may, by notification make rules to carry out the purposes of this regulation.

(2) In particular, and without prejudice to the generality of the foregoing power, such rules may provide for the form in which, the conditions and restrictions subject to which, and the fee not exceeding rupees fifty on payment of which, a pass under section 7 shall be granted.

11. The provisions of this Regulation and of any rule made thereunder shall have effect notwithstanding anything inconsistent there with contained in any other law for the time being in force or any instrument having effect by virtue of any such law, or in any usage or agreement, or in any decree or order of any court or other authority.

Rajendra Prasad, President

K.Y. Bhandarkar, Secretary to the Government of India

By Order

Ram Saran Das, Assistant Secretary (Judicial) to the Chief Commissioner, A&N Islands *Included all amendments until 2004 (Source:UNESCO.2010.The Jarawa Tribal Reserve Dossier: Cultural & Biological Diversities in the Andaman Islands. Edited by Pankaj Sekhsaria and Vishvajit Pandya : UNESCO)

ANNEXURE II

Policy on Jarawa Tribe of Andaman Islands

Published by Authority
No 210, Port Blair, Tuesday, December 21, 2004

I. Introduction

The High Court of Calcutta (Circuit Bench at Port Blair) vide their order dated 09-04-2001 in WP No.048 of 1999 (PIL)- Ms Shyamali Ganguli, Advocate Vs Union of India and Others, inter-alia, directed the Central Government as under :

"The Central Government through the Principal Secretary, Ministray of Home Affairs, within two months from the communication of this order shall form a committee of Experts with the Lt.Governor of the Islands as the Convener, comprising of renowned Anthropologists, Sociologists, Nutrition Experts, Doctors for immediately undertaking a scientific study, research and survey in the aforesaid change in the behavior of the Jarawas and to find out the cause of the same...

The said committee shall submit its report within six months from the formation of such Committee before the Central Government and Lt. Governor, A&N Islands and also shall file a copy thereof before the Circuit Bench of this court.

Within six months thereafter the Central Government through the Home Secretary himself and the Lt. Governor of the Andaman & Nicobar Administration shall formulate a policy, plans and programmes on the aforesaid questions whether the steps should now be taken for bringing the Jarawas in the mainstream of the society or they should be left to their own way of life as before or the balance between the two should be struck following the peaceful existence theory as suggested by Mr. Awaradi in his Master Plan or any other experts. For the aforesaid purpose, the Central Government shall arrange seminars and open discussions of the different experts, National and International on the line, Anthropologists, Sociologists and others as also individuals and non-government organizations having knowledge and experience in the matter inviting them by issuing public notification in widely circulated newspapers and sending them letters of invitation and thereafter shall frame the policy decision within the stipulated period after deliberation and discussion on such opinions with the approval of the concerned Ministry. The Central Government shall also publish the papers, discussions and deliberation of such seminar, at its cost, for future reference....

After formulation of such policy, the same shall be notified by the Central Government and the A&N Administration and shall also be placed before the Circuit Bench of this Hon'ble Court for appropriate order".

2. In pursuance of the aforesaid order of the Hon'ble High Court of Calcutta, a committee of Experts was constituted by the Central Government vide the Ministry of Home Affairs' Notification No. U-14040/24/99-ANL dated the 21st July 2001.

3. The Committee of Experts submitted its report before the Hon'ble High Court of Calcutta on 28-7-2003. As per the aforesaid directions of the Hon'ble High Court, the Central Government was required to formulate policy, plans and programmes in respect of Jarawas in consultation with the Lt. Governor, A&N Islands after organizing seminars and open discussions with the different experts, national and international, Anthropologists, Sociologists and other as also individuals and non-governmental organizations having knowledge nd experience in the matter. Accordingly, the Central Government organized two seminars one at Kolkata on 7-8 April, 2004 and another at Port Blair on 27-28

May,2004 wherein experts, non-government organizations and individuals deliberated on various issues relating to the Jarawas and their well being.

4. The Central Government in the Ministry of Home Affairs considered the report of Committee of Experts vis-à-vis the views that emerged during the two seminars/open discussions organized by the Central Government on the said report of the Expert Committee in consultation with the A&N Administration and the Ministry of Tribal Affairs, the administrative Ministry for the matters connected with tribes and tribal affairs.

5. The Central Government in the Ministry of Home Affairs have consequently decided to frame a policy/ guidelines for the protection and welfare of the Jarawas in Andaman & Nicobar Islands with the following objectives in view:

II. Objectives

(i) To protect the Jarawas from harmful effects of exposures and contact with the outside world while they are not physically, socially and culturally prepared for such interface.

(ii) To preserve the social organization, mode of subsistence and cultural identity of the Jarawa community.

(iii) To provide medical help to the Jarawas to reduce mortality and morbidity in case of their sudden affliction with diseases which their systems are unaccustomed to;

(iv) To conserve the ecology and environment of the Jarawa Reserve Territory and strengthen support systems in order to enable the Jarawas pursue their traditional modes of subsistence and way of life; and

(v) To sensitize settler communities around the Jarawas habitat and personnel working for the protection and preservation of the Jarawas about the need to preserve this ancient community and to value their unique culture and life styles.

III. Strategies/Guidelines

The Central Government with the above objectives in view have framed the following strategies/guidelines for the protection and welfare of the Jarawas.

1. *Protection of Cultural Identity*

(a) The Jarawa shall be considered and treated as a unique human heritage.

(b) A policy of maximum autonomy to the Jarawas with minimum and regulated intervention shall be adopted by the government towards the Jarawas. There shall be no intervention in cultural life of the Jarawas and they will be left at liberty to develop according to their own genius and at their own pace. No attempts to bring them to the mainstream society against their conscious will or to rehabilitate them in separate islands/locations at this stage of their social development will be made.

(c) The quality of intervention with Jarawas will be managed with care and sensitivity through suitably trained and re-oriented personnel, in consultation with and evaluation by anthropologists and experts. The objective will be to avoid dependency syndrome and to ensure their development as a vibrant social group. The personnel working for Jarawas would be provided with proper training and sensitization. The people of the villages near the Jarawa reserve area and other non-tribals will be sensitized regarding the rights and privileges of the Jarawas.

2. *Protection of the Natural Habitat*

(a) No exploitation of natural resources within the Jarawa reserve by any non-tribal including Government agencies will be allowed. Necessary measures shall be initiated to curb even occasional extraction of resources from the Jarawa territory by the non-Jarawas. Provisions of A&N Islands (Protection of Aboriginal Tribes) Regulation, 1956 will be enforced more effectively. The A & N Islands (Protection of Aboriginal Tribes) Regulation 1956, shall be amended to provide stringent punishment for poaching in the Jarawas territory and for exploitation of the Jarawas.

(b) The notified Jarawa territory shall be fully and effectively demarcated and no attempt to curtail, reduce or to acquire land there from shall be made.

(c) All encroachments in the Jarawa territory shall be removed on priority basis. Stringent arrangements to ensure that such encroachments do not take place in future will also be made.

(d) Permanent residence of Government employees/ non-tribals in the Jarawa reserve will not be allowed.

(e) It shall be ensured that no person other than a Jarawa is allowed to enter the notified Jarawa reserve by any means unless he/she is permitted by the competent authority designated by the A&N Administration for this purpose. However no such permission shall be granted unless the person is proceeding on bonafide work relating to the welfare of the Jarawas or protection of the area.

(f) No tourist will be allowed to visit / interact with the Jarawas so that curious intrusions are avoided as these intrusions adversely affect their life style and health.

3. *Protection of Health Status*

(a) Periodic health survey of the Jarawa community will be organized through a Standing Team of health professionals. Only cases needing intensive care will be brought to the hospital but they will be kept in separate enclosures. Appropriate food will be provided instead of the hospital meals. Whenever female Jarawas come or are brought to hospital, female police will be posted invariably.

(b) Medical intervention among the Jarawas i.e. the line of treatment, use of drugs and medicines will be only on the basis of advice of experts in the relevant fields and shall be administered only when found absolutely necessary.

(c) Medical assistance to Jarawas will be extended in their reserve area by qualified health officials as far as feasible so that all the advantages of such in-situ treatment are available to the Jarawas. Jarawa patients will be shifted to hospital only if in-situ treatment is not possible or not felt adequate to save the patient.

(d) The traditional knowledge of the Jarawas including ethno-medicines shall be preserved and documented.

(e) Diagnostic approach, treatment regimen and prescription of drugs in case of common pattern of diseases observed amongst the Jarawas shall be standardized and documented so that experimentation by individual doctors and conflicting assessments can be avoided.

(f) Periodic nutritional and food security surveys shall be conducted to ensure that there is adequate provision of food resources to the Jarawas and that there is no fall in nutritional standards.

(g) The Jarawas shall not be provided food which is alien to their normal dietary habits.

(h) Officials/workers engaged in protection and welfare of the Jarawas will be regularly screened to ensure that they are absolutely free from any communicable disease and they do not encourage addictive habits such as smoking and drinking amongst the Jarawa population.

IV. Regulation of Traffic on Andaman Trunk Road

(a) Traffic on Andaman Trunk Road will be regulated strictly limiting the traffic to the essential purposes of public transport, supplies and emergency evacuation of patients and to ensure that it is an innocent and harmless passage and not a source of trouble to the Jarawas.

(b) Vehicles on Andaman Trunk Road will be allowed to move only in restricted hours and in convoy under notified speed limit to avert possible road accidents and to avoid any sort of interaction of travelers with Jarawas.

(c) Facilities for travel by boat /ship will be strengthened and transportation /travel by sea will be encouraged.

(d) Maintenance of the Andaman Trunk Road will be carried out by a mobile maintenance team bringing men, machine and materials from Ferrargunj/ Jirkatang and carry out the job only during day time.

(e) The tourist traffic on Andaman Trunk Road will be strictly monitored to ensure that there is no interaction between the Jarawas and the tourists.

V. Codification of Jarawa Language

(a) Codification of the language of Jarawas shall be done with the advice and involvement of experts. However, continuous interaction in the name of codification of language will not be allowed. Codification of language shall be attempted be relevant experts in a discreet manner during periodical health surveys of the Jarawas.

(b) Officials of the A&N Administration who will be coming in contact with the Jarawas particularly those of Health and welfare departments will be encouraged to learn the Jarawa language so that they are able to communicate with them and understand their perceptions, reactions and problems.

VI. Institutional Arrangements

(a) The A&N Administration shall be wholly and entirely responsible for the implementation of the aforesaid policy on the Jarawas. It shall lay down detailed tasks for each agency and unit of the administrative machinery and set up structures for monitoring and specific mechanism for enforcing accountability of officials in respect of tasks assigned to them in connection with protection and welfare of the Jarawas.

(b) The Andaman Adim Janjati Vikas Samiti (AAJVS) an autonomous body will function like a trustee of the interest of the Jarawas and advise A&N Administration regarding the protection and welfare of all aboriginal tribes including the Jarawas.

(c) The Executive Council of the AAJVS assisted by experts and persons having knowledge and experience in tribal affairs under the chairmanship of Lt. Governor will enforce and monitor implementation of the policy.

(d) Meaningful research on the Jarawas will be allowed under the advice of AAJVS to further understanding of their life and culture including their traditional knowledge. However, it shall be ensured strictly that the confidentiality of genetic resources on thye Jarawas will be maintained and not used for commercial exploitation by any agency or organization which is not directly concerned with the welfare and protection of the Jarawas.

(e) Periodic review of this policy will be done so that the policy is dynamic and takes into account changing needs and circumstances.

ANNEXURE III (A)

The Periodical Notifications of the Jarawa Reserve in South Andaman

Notification	*Area (South Andaman)*
1	*2*
Notification in The Andaman and Nicobar Gazette, Extraordinary published by Authority on Tuesday, 2nd April 1957	The area in South Andaman to the west of an imaginary boundary line starting north-eastwards from the mouth of constance Bay along Bajalungta Jig to the southern trip of Cholunga Range and then proceeding northwards to Mount Cadell and from there eastward to Pochang Creek and thence along the eastern coast of South Andaman Island proceeding to point 600228 (omitting James, Kyd and other islands and islets) and thence from that point northwards along an alignment to be aligned by the Andaman and Nicobar Islands Forest department taking into consideration the suitability of terrain and water points to join Putatang Jig and thence northwards along Putatang Jig and Amitla Boicha Pasaage of Middle Strait along the east coast of South Andaman excluding Belle Island, Bonig Island, Oral Kalcha and Baby Island proceeding to Yeratil Jig via Needam Beach and Port Anson enclosing Bluff and Spike Islands.

(Contd...)

1	*2*
Notification in The Andaman and Nicobar Gazette, Extraordinary published by Authority on Thursday, 19th July 1979(Amending the previous notification)	The part of South Andaman Island situated in the west of the imaginary boundary line including coastal water upto 3 Km starting from the mouth of Constance Bay proceeds north upto north west corner of village Tirur and thence proceeds towards east-north and joins Andaman Trunk Road at a point 2Km south of Miletilak from where the boundary proceeds towards north upto Middle Strait point along the western side of the Andaman Trunk Road having a 200 meter belt excluding village areas of Miletilak and all allotted land of Jirkatang area. From Middle Strait point the boundary proceeds towards north via Needham Beach, enclosing Bluff and Spike Islands to Yeratil Jig.
Andaman & Nicobar Adminstration Notification No 1-467/86-TW dated 2nd November 1989.	The 'Jarawa Reserve' as notified in 1979 above includes the Survey No 2265/5 area measuring 1000sq.mts situated at Aberdeen Village, Port Blair, Andaman District.
The Andaman & Nicobar Administration Notification No 159/2004/F.NO/1-752/ 2002-TW (PF) dated 15th September 2004 (In supersession of the Administration's Notification of 19th July 1979 and Notification	The part of South Andaman Island situated in the west of the imaginary boundary line starting from the mouth of Constance Bay (East Longitude 92 degree 34'03" and North Latitude 11 degree 39'52") proceeds towards north up to mouth of Banjlungtajig (East Longitude 92 degree 35'20" and

(Contd...)

1	*2*
No 1-324/82-TW dated 09/04/1984)	North Latitude 11 degree 42'18") and proceeds towards east through the mangrove swamp and meets a point (East Longitude 92 degree 36'26" and North Latitude 11 degree 42'31"). Then the boundary proceeds North and follows the ridge (East Longitude 92 degree 36'26" and North Latitude 11 degree 43'51") and meets a point (East Longitude 92 degree 36'59" and North Latitude 11 degree 44'25") and then boundary turns South-East and proceeds through a point (East Longitude and 92 degree 37'20" North Latitude 11 degree 44'15") and further proceeds towards North through a point (East Longitude 92 degree 37'46" and North Latitude 11 degree 46'14") and thence proceeds towards North-East and joins a point 30 M West of center line of Andaman Trunk Road at milestone of 52 Kms point on Chidiatapu to Middle Strait Andaman Trunk Road, from where the boundary proceeds alongside the Andaman Trunk Road excluding area of Mile Tilak village and all allotted land of Jirkatang area up to the milestone of 61 Kms. The boundary then turns towards east and follows the ridge of 100 M height point (East Longitude 92 degree 40'10" and North Latitude 11 degree 51'35") and proceeds

(Contd...)

1	*2*
	further South-East and passes through the 123 M height ridge (East Longitude 92 degree 41'02" and North Latitude 11 degree 51'12") and further proceeds South-East and meets a point (East Longitude 92 degree 42'26" and North Latitude 11 degree 50'11") and finally joins Mangrove Creek at point (East Longitude 92 degree 42'15" and North Latitude 11 degree 49'57") and afterwards follows through the mangrove creek and then western bank of Shoal Bay Creek and thereafter proceeds North along the eastern coast of South Andaman Island (excluding James, Kyd, other islands and islets) and follows Amitla Boicha Passage and then follows southern bank of Middle Strait Jetty/harbour, Belle Island, Boning Island, Oralkatcha, Baby Island, Stoat Island and Talakaicha Island. Then the boundary follows Middle Starit towards north wards via Needham beach passage, enclosing Bluff and Spike Island and then follows Homfray's Strait up to Yeratiljig Creek mouth.

ANNEXURE III(B)

The Periodical Notifications of the Jarawa Reserve in Middle Andaman

Notification	*Area (Middle Andaman)*
1	*2*
Notification in The Andaman and Nicobar Gazette, Extraordinary published by Authority on Tuesday, 2nd April 1957	The area in Middle Andaman to the west of an imaginary line emerging from South Andaman and proceeding towards Yeratil Jig to Ranger's Channel along the Bush Police Line subject to an adjustment that the line may coincide with an alignment to be aligned with Andaman Nicobar Islands Forest Department in Porlob and Yol areas between the Yeratil Charalungta Bush Police posts provide that sufficient land is left to the west of such alignment on the west side of the range to provide enough hunting ground to Jarawa so that they are on the move and bearing in mind the suitability of the alignment, from the point of view of water and terrain, as their path.
Notification (of ammendment) dated 1st Decemeber 1959	The area in Middle Andaman to the west of an imaginary line emerging from South Andaman and proceeding towards Yeratiljig to Bush Police Post No 4 (Map reference 772425) and thence due west to the coast below point June (Map reference 625029) along the Bush Police line subject to an adjustment that the line may coincide with the alignment to be

(Contd...)

1	*2*
	aligned by the Andaman and Nicobar Islands Forest Department in Porlob and Boroin Yol areas between the Yeratil/ Charalungta Bush Police posts provided that sufficient land is left to the west of such alignment on the eastern side of the Range to provide enough hunting ground to Jarawas while they are on the move and bearing in mind the suitability of such alignment from the point of view of water and terrain, as a petrol path.
Notification in The Andaman and Nicobar Gazette, Extraordinary published by Authority on Thursday, 19th July 1979 (Amending the previous notification)	The part of Middle Andaman Islands situated in the western side of the imaginary boundary line including coastal water upto 3 Km starting from Yeratil Jig and proceeds towards north-east excluding village areas of Kadamtala and touches Andaman Trunk Road at a point 12 Km north of Uttara Jetty and passes alongside the road leaving 200 metres belt upto 24 Km point of the Andaman Trunk Road from Uttara Jetty and thence due north through jungle upto a distance of 6 Km and then towards north-east from a distance of 7 Km and further proceeds due north of 11 Km and joins Wolaga Boilu Creek. Thereafter the boundary line proceeds north-west through the boundary Wolaga Boilu Creek

(Contd...)

1	*2*
	upto the point 1/3 Km from the northern tip of the village Hanspuri and around south-west and southern side keeping the same half a Km distance from village Hanspuri extending and culminating ultimately at Bush Police Camp No 32 facing the Luice Inlet including entire Wolaga Boilu, Melagar Boilu and Mar Boilu Creeks.
The Andaman & Nicobar Administration Notification No 159/2004/F.NO/1-752/2002-TW (PF) dated 15th September 2004 (In supersession of the Administration's Notification of 19th July 1979 and Notification No 1-324/82-TW dated 09/04/1984)	From the above point namely the mouth of Yeratiljig creek (East Longitude 92 degree 44' and North Latitude 12 degree 18'23") boundary in Middle Andaman follows Yeratiljig Creek along western bank excluding village area of Kadamtala and boundary finally meeting milestone of 142 Kms on ATR (i.e. 12 Kms milestone from Uttara Jetty). Then it follows the ATR leaving 30 M from the center line of road upto 24 Km point of the Andaman Trunk Road from Uttara Jetty and thence the boundary follows the ridge of 100 M height point (East Longitude 92 degree 47'20" and North Latitude 12 degree 30'), ridge of 104 M height point (East Longitude 92 degree 47'55" and North Latitude 12 degree 31'10"), ridge of 122 M height point (East Longitude 92 degree 48'21" and North Latitude 12 degree 32'24"), ridge of 168 M height (East

(Contd...)

1	*2*
	Longitude 92 degree 48'28" and North Latitude 12 degree 32'45"), ridge of 122 M height point (East Longitude 92 degree 49'02" and North Latitude 12 degree 33'39"), ridge of 125 M height point (East Longitude 92 degree 50'34" and North Latitude 12 degree 35'50"), ridge of 132 M height point (East Longitude 92 degree 50'21" and North Latitude 12 degree 36'45") and meets the origin of Picher Nallah (East Longitude 92 degree 50'28" and North Latitude 12 degree 37'33", i.e. the old Kalsi 4 No. JPP). Then the boundary follows towards Northwards following the ridge of 68 M height point (East Longitude 92 degree 50'23" and North Latitude 12 degree 38'37"), ridge of 73 M height point (East Longitude 92 degree 50'17" and North Latitude 12 degree 39'48") then turns North-East and follows the ridge of 194 M height point (East Longitude 92 degree 51'10" and North Latitude 12 degree 41'55") and then the boundary turns to North-West and passes through the ridge of 201 M height point (East Longitude 92 degree 49'30" and North Latitude 12 degree 42'48") and ridge of 100 M height point (East Longitude 92 degree 48'40" and North Latitude 12 degree 43'05") and meets the Chain pur Nallah in mangrove

(Contd...)

1	2
	swamp at a point (East Longitude 92 degree 48'06" and North Latitude 12 degree 43'14") then proceeds towards west through Chainpur Nallah and meets a point having East Longitude 92 degree 47'02" and North Latitude 12 degree 43'27" and then boundary follows southwards through the mangrove swamp following western bank of Chainpur Nallah and finally meets sea through Lewis Inlet. The existing belt of 200 metres from the central line of Andaman Trunk Road, on either side is restricted to 30 metres on either side of the ATR except at Nilambur-Middle Strait and Uttara-Gandhighat where the existing jetty and port facilities will continue to be outside the reserved area. The above reserve is also extended to coastal waters up to a distance of 5 Km from the high tide line on the western side of the South and Middle Andaman Islands from Constance Bay to Lewis Inlet Bay.

MAPS

Traditional Route of Jarawa Movement

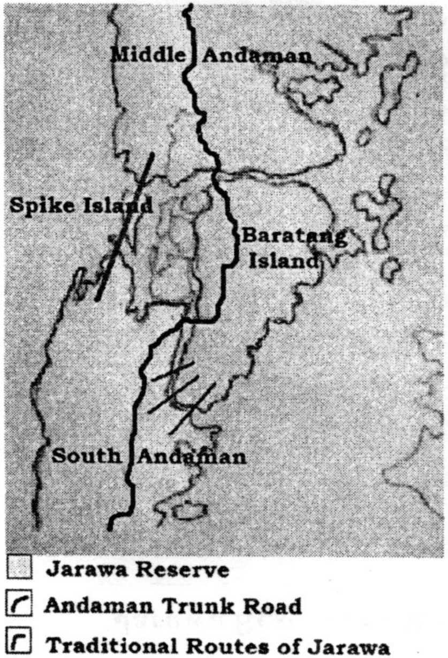

Old Map of Jarawa Reserve in Middle Andaman

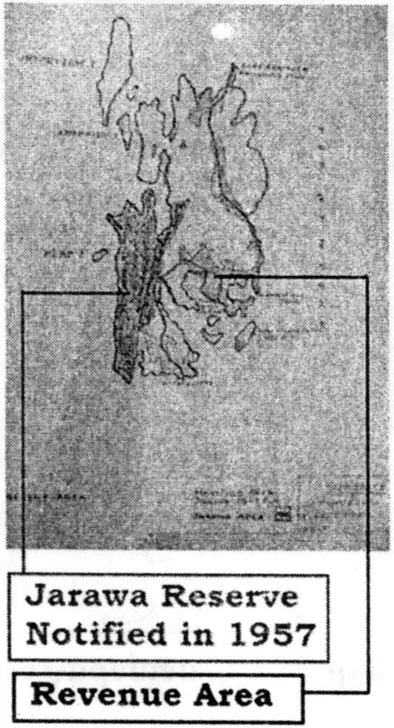

Old Map of Jarawa Reserve in South Andaman

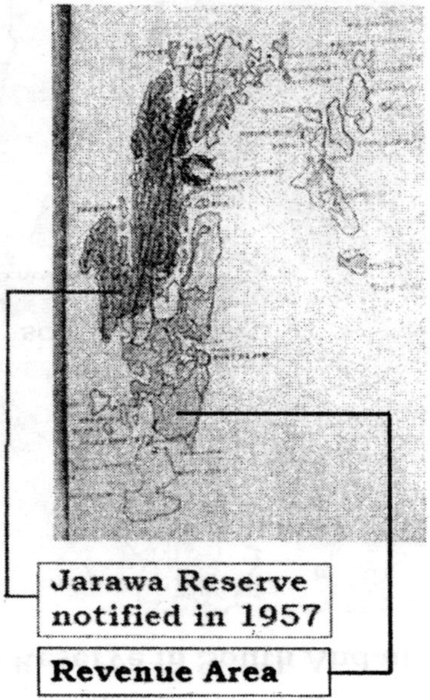

Jarawa Reserve in Middle Andaman

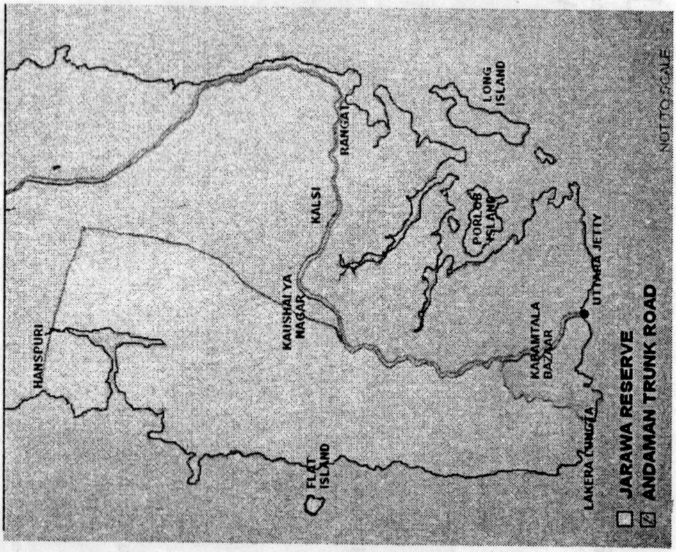

Jarawa Reserve in South Andaman

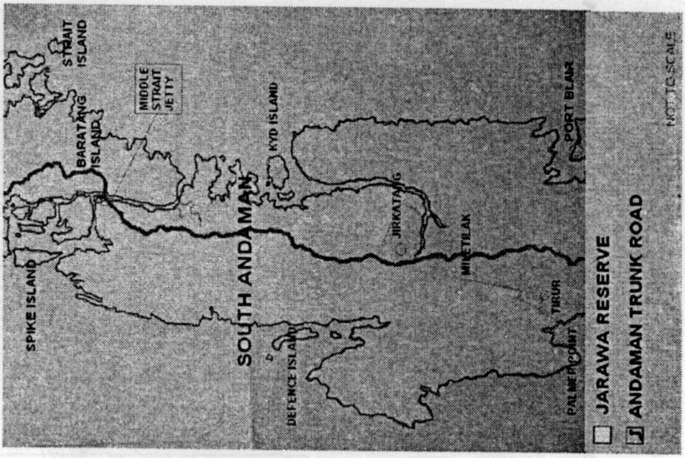

Jarawa Reserve Notified in Andaman Islands

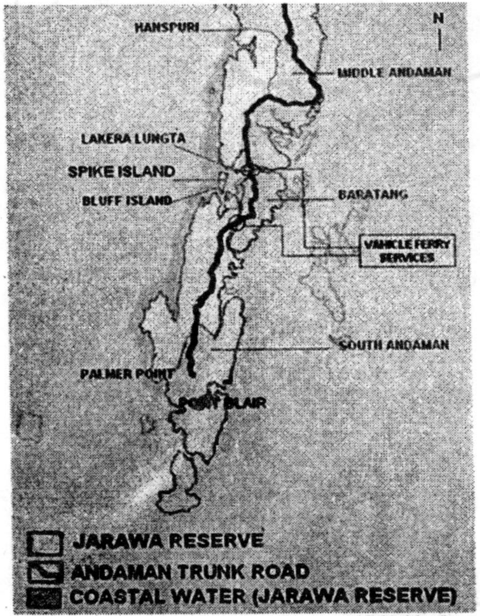

NOT TO SCALE

ATR obstructing Jarawa Access to Creeks and Water Bodies

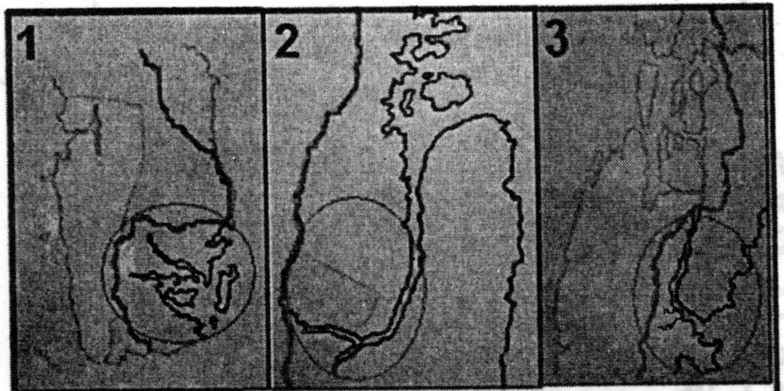

1 Yoljig Creek, Boroinjig Creek, Porlobjig Creek and region around Porlob Island (Middle Andaman)

2 Jirkatanag Creek, Putatangjig Creek and region around Kyd Island (South Andaman)

3 Amitla Boicha Passage and region around Baratang Island (South Andaman)

SKETCHES

THE JARAWA ARTICLES

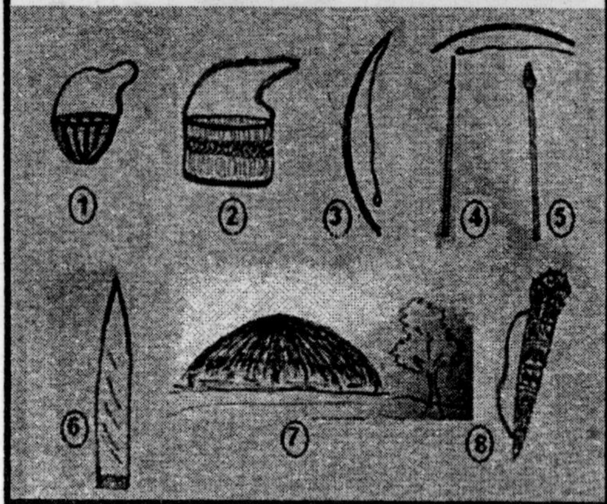

1. Cane basket 2. Honey Tub 3. Bow 4. Fishing arrow 5. Hunting Arrow 6. traditional knife (Towa) 7. Community hut 8. Resin Torch

LOCATION OF KADAMTALA REGION ADJACENT TO JARAWA RESERVE

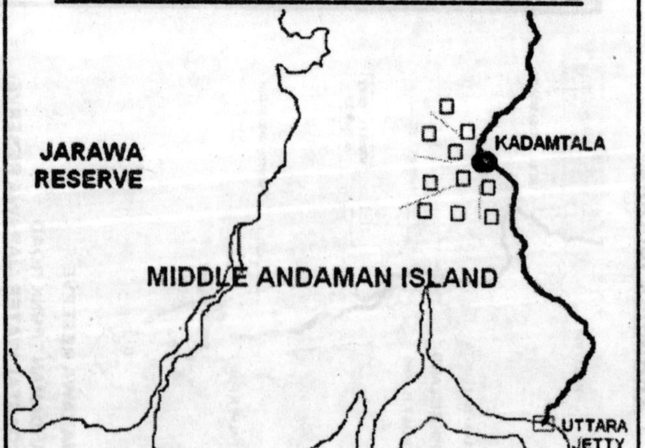

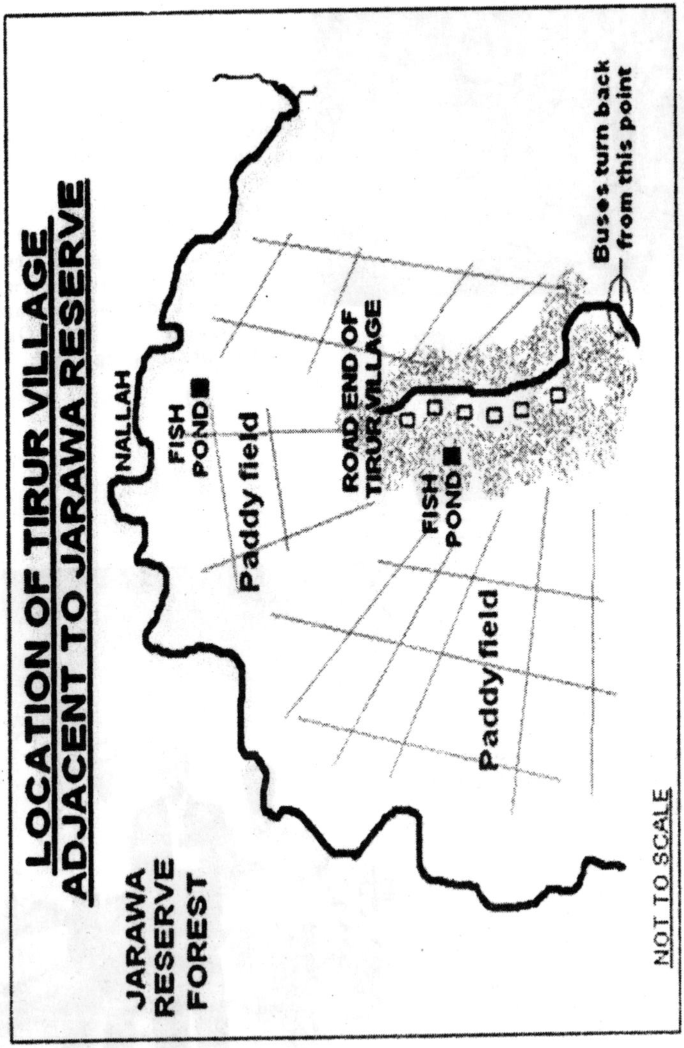
LOCATION OF TIRUR VILLAGE
ADJACENT TO JARAWA RESERVE
JARAWA
RESERVE
FOREST
NALLAH
FISH
POND
Paddy field
ROAD END OF
TIRUR VILLAGE
FISH
POND
Paddy field
Buses turn back
from this point
NOT TO SCALE

PLATES

Pieces of Onge pots (called 'Wey' in Onge language) unearthed from a kitchen midden of their community hut namely 'Tambebui Beyra' near Onge settlement at Dugong Creek in 2007 by the author, who then worked as Research Investigator in the Onge settlement, Dugong Creek.

The Author with Onge couple in front of the Taj Mahal at Agra in 2009

From Left Smt. Kakae (Onge), Shri GB Mukherjee, Secretary to Govt of India, Ministry of Tribal Affairs, Shri Tai (Onge), Author as Escort to Tribal Guests and two staffs of MTA at New Delhi.

On the Spike Island (Jarawa Reserve)

A Jarawa Woman

Three Negrito tribesmen at one place

Index